TOMÁS IBÁÑEZ

ANARCHISM
IS MOVEMENT

ANARCHISM IS MOVEMENT

by Tomás Ibáñez
with foreword by
Peter Gelderloos

Translated by
the Autonomies Collective

Edited by
Rob Ray and Scorsby

This edition published by
Freedom Press, 2019
84b Whitechapel High St,
London E1 7QX

ISBN 978-1-904491-33-0

Designed by
Euan Monaghan

Printed in the UK by
Imprint Digital

FOREWORD

by Peter Gelderloos

In *Anarchism is Movement* Tomás Ibañez offers several straightforward affirmations about anarchism to make sense of its renovation and resurgence at the end of the 20th century, and to identify the potential advantages it brings to the struggles of the 21st. These affirmations include the necessary simultaneity of theory and practice at the heart of anarchism, and the ethical preoccupation with fighting power in all its manifestations. Taken together, these characteristics mean that anarchism cannot — and will not — be a corpus of philosophy and doctrine that updates itself, if at all, through occasional theoretical revisions its disciples will squabble over for decades. This is the fate of those movements that put their claim to some singular truth before their commitment to the struggle for liberation. On the contrary, anarchism is constantly reborn through its practice, constantly adapting to the way power is constituted in a specific historical moment. Though we can identify many of the same principles, ideas, and methods from the 19th century to today, there are also undeniable differences in how anarchists think and act, corresponding in large part to the vast changes that have taken place in the society at large, within which and against which we struggle.

This is relevant, for Ibañez, in light of a series of criticisms directed by those he terms the "temple guards" against innovative — or unorthodox — characteristics of the newly renovated anarchism of today. It's not a mass movement, it's too subcultural, it's lost its class focus, it's just a lifestyle, it's too insurrectional, it's not serious about building large, permanent organisations. These defenders of a "mummified" anarchism can't have it both ways, argues Ibañez: they can't rejoice in the rebirth of anarchism while also negating the very features that allowed it to flourish in the new sociopolitical and cultural context.

It might help readers of the English translation to know that these temple guards certainly left their mark on the last few decades of Spanish anarchism. After experiencing the heyday of one of the strongest anarchist movements in the world, a partial revolution in 1936, and then a bloody defeat in the Spanish Civil War, the veterans of the movement fled, mostly to France, where they passed 40 years or more in exile, slowly dying off, many of them disconnected from the once powerful movements they had helped create as the entire world was cast under the shadow of the Cold War, a contest between two authoritarian, brutal powers that stamped out any imaginary of a meaningful liberation. This is a reality Tomás Ibañez knows only too well.

Ibañez never makes his arguments personal, but I think it worth mentioning that those who managed to hold onto control of the glorified CNT[1] in exile, though they did set themselves up as "guardians of the temple", were far from orthodox themselves. In fact, they broke with the most fundamental of anarchist orthodoxies — opposition to the State — when they joined the Republican government late in 1936, opening the way for the Stalinists to crush the revolution long before the fascists won the war in 1939. Likewise, these mummies were some of the first to

---

[1] The Confederación Nacional del Trabajo was at its height the largest anarchist organisation in history. The anarcho-syndicalist union was a key player in the Spanish Civil War of 1936-39.

use the argument that a women's struggle would divide the movement or take the focus off the class struggle: they started saying this way back in February 1936 when they tried to prevent the creation of Mujeres Libres, a group of anarchist women that remained far more radical and principled throughout the Civil War than the higher committees of the CNT. And while it's true that more anarchists today emphasise the struggle against patriarchy, racism, and colonialism, fortunately we can find examples of the same going back to the 19th century.

Nonetheless, when these mummies went back to Spain in the '70s, towards the end of the Franco dictatorship, they tried to impose their unorthodox orthodoxies at great cost to the growing movement. Many anarchists like Tomás Ibañez or Salvador Puig Antich gladly worked in diverse, revolutionary circles, joining their anarchism to the dissident Marxism, council communism, autonomism and other currents practiced by their comrades within the powerful wildcat strike movement that helped bring an end to the regime. As the Comisiones Obreras—the Workers' Commissions—came under the control of the authoritarian communists and then entered into dialogue with the State, the CNT grew quickly. Another revolutionary moment was on the horizon. But the leaders of the CNT did not want to share power in the organisation with these new (and sometimes not so new) currents. They wanted the tens of thousands of young workers and unemployed to join the organisation, but not to transform it. They squabbled for power, and the organisation just as quickly fell apart.

The guardians of the temple didn't disappear. Their refusal to support anarchist expropriators in 1996 is connected to another schism and the birth of insurrectionary anarchism in Spain (in its present form, in any case, as there were also strong insurrectionary currents within the CNT in the 1920s and '30s).

Even though this mummified anarchism left its clearest mark in Spain, we can often hear its voice in other countries as well, even anglophone countries where very few older anarchists remain in touch with the movement. In these places, younger anarchists call out for a return to classical anarchism, often inspiring themselves, ironically, with a romanticised version of the Spanish Civil War. They fail to realise that it was not fascism that killed the anarchist revolution in some heroic and pure, albeit doomed, struggle; this was only the case in places like Andalucía and Extremadura that fell early in the war. Rather, it was the syndicalist leadership itself, wielding a knife provided by the Stalinists. Drawing a clean historical lesson from this bloody episode becomes even more difficult when we acknowledge that the revolution only became a possibility in the first place thanks to a militant anarcho-syndicalism with strong insurrectionary tendencies. What's the correct strategy, if the movement's strength turned into its weakness?

Among English-speakers, the most well known text calling for a return to a mythical classical anarchism is Murray Bookchin's less-than-honest *Social Anarchism vs Lifestyle Anarchism: An Unbridgeable Chasm*. Ibañez handily dismantles the unfortunate dichotomy at the heart of this book, which marks Bookchin's own descent into mummified authoritarianism[2]. To complement Ibañez's logical argument, I would provide a practical example. From the UK to Greece and beyond, disaffected and marginalised youth in the '70s, '80s, and '90s turned their noses at the austere Communist Party and flocked to the rock 'n roll—or more specifically the punk—scene, in which anarchism was one of the few subversive theories to achieve some intelligible articulation amidst all the grunting and repetitive guitar chords. As a practice, anarchism combined perfectly with the ethos of DIY, seizure of autonomous spaces that were disruptive at least at a cultural level, and rejection of bourgeois morals

---

2   Ed's note: Bookchin (1921-2006) was a defining figure in the development of social ecology, a green left libertarian approach to social transformation, and remains highly respected for his early work, but his later legacy, including a bitter conflict with what he regarded as the lifestylist wing of anarchism, is heavily debated.

and authorities. The Communist Party taught respect for a new set of authorities and some very old doctrines, and it withered to irrelevance. Anarchism lent itself to a new generation to express what they thought was wrong with the world, and it flourished.

Did punk facilitate a superficial understanding of anarchism? Probably. Did it have a tendency towards commercialisation and selling out from the very beginning? Without a doubt. Was it an appropriate vehicle for inviting any type of person into the movement? It never claimed to be. Could anarchism possibly have gotten a better start, coming out of a decades-long eclipse after being brutally repressed by both Left and Right and forgotten by most of the planet? Maybe not.

In sum, we can criticise punk anarchism, but Ibañez would say it doesn't make any sense to negate it while celebrating the resurgence of anarchism as a whole, especially when the changes we might see as weaknesses in this new anarchism represent changes in how capitalist society functions at a global level.

Case in point: who doesn't see the romance in imagining themselves part of an anarchist union with millions of members, unifying everyone who has to work for a living against the bosses? But is it realistic to propose a mass movement when capitalism has already replaced a mass society with a hyper-atomised society in which power flows are much more networked? We mustn't forget that "mass" and "large" or "numerous" are not exact synonyms.

Just as urban masses were the result of social control techniques that got rid of the earlier rural communities, and these in turn were imprinted by even earlier techniques of control, the masses have been dissolved and atomised by spectacular media, individualised communications technology, changing urban design and architecture, greater precarity in the economy, and a thousand other concerted movements. The masses don't exist anymore, which might explain why today, "revolutionary mass organisations" tend to be smaller than your average network of affinity groups.

Reading about Makhno, Marusya[3], and Kim Chwa-jin[4], we might really be taken by the idea of peasant communes and militias, but no one who lives in an industrialised consumer economy in the UK or the US is going to advocate that as a serious revolutionary strategy.

This is Ibañez's strength. He embraces change, he identifies the ideas that hold us back, without ever abandoning that which would constitute the spirit of anarchism, if he believed in such a thing: the hopeful, bold, utopian, practical struggle against domination. In arguing against some timeless, eternal anarchist movement, Ibañez delivers an effective critique of essentialism, one of modernity's most persistent structures, making a comeback today on the Right and the Left (for an incredibly moving, astute critique of essentialism that is both contemporary and historically grounded, I recommend *The Unquiet Dead: Anarchism, Fascism, and Mythology*). And while discussing both the merits and some criticisms of post-anarchism or post-structuralist anarchism, Ibañez forms an excellent synthesis between Foucault's[5] correct but potentially defeatist analysis of power being reproduced everywhere and anarchism's ethical insistence on fighting power wherever we find it.

By clearly exposing these different theoretical concerns, Ibañez helps us "understand what underpins our thought, practices, subjectivities and libertarian sensibilities. Such understanding may help to better focus our struggles against domination". Even if you disagree with some of his evaluations, you will benefit from how he frames the debate.

---

3   Nestor Makhno (1888-1934) and Marusya (1885-1919) were legendary leading figures in the Ukranian anarchist revolution of 1918-1921. The Free Territory, which covered a population of nearly seven million, resisted both the White and Red armies while attempting to institute a system of free communes.
4   Kim Chwa-chin (1889-1930) was a famous anti-imperialist and leader of the anarchist rebel forces of Shinmin, Manchuria in 1929.
5   Michel Foucault was one of the most important philosophers of the 20th century. His theories of how power is affected in modern society, particularly in *Discipline and Punish*, have impacted on many aspects of anarchist thinking.

TRANSLATORS' NOTES

Tomás Ibáñez's essay was first published in Spanish in 2014 by Virus Editorial. Among our motives for undertaking this translation of his work, there is first the desire to share with English speakers the work of anarchist writers and militants from the Spanish speaking world and, secondly, in this instance (and by no means the first time), to share the work of Tomás Ibáñez, with whom we have great affinity.

The life of Tomás Ibáñez was marked by anarchism from his childhood. The son of a Spanish libertarian exile in France, he participated, in the 1960s, in the also-exiled Federación Ibérica de Juventudes Libertarias (FIJL). In 1968 he joined the March 22 Movement[6], participating actively in the May events of that year, until his arrest in June, and subsequent forced "internal exile" outside Paris. In 1973, upon the death of dictator Francisco Franco, he returned to Spain and participated in attempts to rebuild the Spanish CNT.

Activist, journalist, essayist, academic, Ibáñez's voice within anarchism remains among the most creative. For more check out autonomies.org/tag/tomas-ibanez.

~ **Autonomies Collective**

---

6 Based at the University of Nanterre, the March 22 Movement was one of the core series of clashes which sparked massive political upheavals in Paris a few months later which became known as the May '68 unrest. Alongside Ibáñez at the time was Daniel Cohn Bendit, or Danny The Red, who became one of the uprising's most recognisable figures.

ANARCHISM IS MOVEMENT

PREAMBLE

Yes! Anarchism is in movement and it is so twice over.

On the one hand, it has thrown itself towards a dynamic of renewal that has it move at a speed that it has not known for a long time and which translates, among other things, into a significant expansion of its forms and themes of intervention, in the strong diversification of the shapes that it takes on and in the considerable increase of its publications.

On the other hand, the social, cultural, political and technological changes that have occurred over these last decades vigorously spur it on and drive it towards a rapid expansion in distinct zones of the world. Anarchist symbols appear in the most remote regions of the globe; anarchist actions show up in the news, where they are least expected, and anarchist movements, whose magnitude is at times surprising, stir up multiple geographical areas.

Should we be happy? Of course! Because, parochial patriotism aside, what is good for anarchism is good for all people who, having heard of anarchism or not, knowing or not what it means and sharing or not its principles, suffer in the flesh domination and exploitation and, in some cases, cherish dreams of revolt and rebelliousness. To taint social and political reality with a little more anarchism cannot but disrupt the smooth running of oppression and injustice.

Does this robust expansion of anarchism herald the coming of a more libertarian and egalitarian society, or at least, a few social transformations of great magnitude? To these questions, the answer can only be: *not by a long shot!* We are no longer at the age of believing in fairy tales and we know perfectly well that, even assuming the number of persons touched by the influence of anarchism has undergone an extraordinary growth, it continues to represent a population of *Lilliputian* dimensions; far too insignificant in the face of the more than 7 billion human beings, of every condition and belief, that inhabit the planet and of whom, it must be believed, a great many would prefer, however difficult it is to accept, other systems of values and other ways of life than those that appear so desirable to us.

However, once the siren's song announcing radiant mornings is silenced and utopian hopes locked away in the trunk of old illusory dreams, what still remains is that the current revival of anarchism is the bearer of excellent prospects for all of the practices of resistance, subversion and rebelliousness that confront the impositions of the reigning social system. The expansion of anarchism opens up the possibility of multiplying and intensifying struggles against the apparatuses of domination, of increasingly putting in check attacks on the dignity and the conditions of life of people, of subverting the social relations moulded by mercantilist logic, of tearing away spaces to live differently, of transforming our subjectivities, of reducing social inequalities and expanding the space open to practices of freedom.

And all of this is not for tomorrow or the day after tomorrow; not for after the great explosion that will change everything, but for today, in the day to day, in the quotidian. For it is in the here and now that the only revolution that exists and is truly lived is carried out, in our practices, in our struggles and in our way of living. Here and now, as Gustav Landauer[7] once indicated when he said "anarchism is not a thing of the future but of the present".

---

7   Gustav Landauer is widely regarded as a classic theorist of social anarchism. Most active in the 1900s-1910s, he was a leading light in the Bavarian Socialist Republic of 1919 and was killed when it was crushed.

To make a mark in the reality where we live, even if not in the whole of it, even if only in a fragmentary way, to have a bearing on it, finally, after so much time of seeing it pass through our fingers like sand and to thus transform it in the present, no doubt in a piecemeal way, but radically, this is what today's anarchism in movement offers us. And this, let us not doubt for a moment, is far from being a little thing, above all when we see that the principles, practices and realisations which characterise anarchism are reinvented, claimed and deployed by collectives and by people who do not necessarily come from milieus that define themselves as such.

I invite you on this occasion to take a brief walk through the resurgence and renewal of anarchism, hoping—as does anyone who writes—that I can awaken your interest and keep your company until the end, even if the path that I have taken, or my way of following it, is not necessarily the most appropriate.

I have considerably lightened the principal body of this text, placing the development of certain themes in a few final *addenda*. They deal with questions that in my view are undoubtedly important, but where detailed analysis is unnecessary to follow the book's principal argument. They can nevertheless be consulted by those desirous of deepening their understanding. The three addenda that I have included address questions of modernity and postmodernity, poststructuralism, and relativism.

Finally, I have to make two clarifications regarding the bibliography. Bibliographic references are usually alphabetised by author name and this is effectively how the general bibliography is presented at the end of the book.

The second clarification is that in writing this book, I turned to many of my own prior texts. It is for this reason that I thought it convenient to have a separate bibliography of my own work that I have used in this book or that maintain a very direct relationship with it.

THE IMPETUOUS RESURGENCE OF
ANARCHISM IN THE BEGINNING
OF THE 21ST CENTURY

Beneath the incredulous gaze of those who had locked it in the dungeons of history and to the surprise of many, anarchism has been experiencing an impressive increase in momentum since the beginning of the 21st century that has manifested itself in various regions of the globe. Independently of whether this worries or inspires, it has to be stated that anarchism occupies once again a significant place on the political scene and that it is in the process of reinventing itself on the triple plane of its practices, theory and social diffusion.

When an unexpected event occurs it is easy to declare after the fact that its mere occurrence is proof that it *had* to happen and anyone well-informed enough could have anticipated it. This is of course not generally the case and, with respect to anarchism, it is clear that the ideology's return onto the political scene could easily not have happened. No historical necessity fueled its resurgence, nor that of any other social phenomenon. Nothing is fated since the beginning and for ever and this is a great good fortune, for this is the price of the very possibility of freedom. Against our idealised images, we have to recognise that if anarchy formed part of humanity's deepest aspirations, if it were etched in some way onto human nature, or, also, if humanity moved necessarily towards a horizon of anarchy, despite the ups and downs of history, paradoxically little space would remain for the *idea* of freedom. Castoriadis[8] saw it clearly. Either the social-historical is open and permits radical creativity, or we are condemned to endlessly repeat what already exists. Hence a choice has to be made between, on the one hand, a conception of historical reality that allows for the possibility of freedom, even though this places the perennity of anarchism at risk and, on the other hand, a conception that can assure, eventually, the permanence of anarchism inscribed at the heart of history, but which reduces the field of freedom considerably.

Refusing to subscribe to theological conceptions of history and rejecting strict historical determinism does not impede us from investigating and analysing the reasons why anarchism rides again. It is precisely these reasons that this book aims to help clarify.

In any case, it is not only a matter of giving *an account* of anarchism, outlining it in its current resurgence, but to contribute to the renewal of its practices and its thought. This book does not have a purely descriptive goal, but is politically *committed* to outlining new ways of conceiving and practicing anarchism. These new ways appear to have a more direct connection with current reality and are in a better position to expand the influence of libertarian ideas. Not because this expansion is good in itself, or should be pursued for its own sake, but because it can only have beneficial consequences for the victims of domination and exploitation.

I warred for some time against the *guardians of the temple*; that is, against those who wanted to preserve anarchism in the exact form that was inherited, as the risk of strangling it and impeding its evolution. My appeals then go back some time for "an anarchism disposed to constantly putting its very foundations at risk, directing towards itself the most irreverent of critical reviews". These exhortations, challenging not classical anarchism but its fossilisation at the hands of the vigilantes of orthodoxy,

---

8 Cornelius Castoriadis (1922-1997) was a founder of the French group Socialism Ou
   Barbarie and one of the most influential libertarian socialist thinkers of the 20th century.

seem to me to be necessary at certain times, though they have ceased to be so today. The exuberant vitality of anarchism has effectively barred those, brimming with love for it, who tried to fix it in amber, so as to preserve it better. The guardians of the temple continue to exist, of course, but they can only carry out rearguard actions and it seems useless and of little interest to develop a critical discourse against their narrow and dusty conception. The concern now is to contribute to stimulating the new anarchism that is developing verdantly, beneath our very gaze. What is important is to help to reform it in the frame of the current epoch, without stopping to criticise this or that aspect of expired conceptions.

To say that anarchism is resurging in the present is to affirm, simultaneously, that it has found itself more or less *missing* for some time. Likewise, when it is stated that anarchism is reinventing itself, it is suggested that this is not *a mere reproduction* of previously existing anarchism, but the incorporation of some innovative aspects. Even though the concern here is not to present its past, the reference to the eventual *eclipse of anarchism* and its supposed withdrawal from the political scene obliges us to cast a glance over its history to see whether this has effectively been so. However, previous to that, I believe that it is useful to reflect on theoretical scenarios where the question of an eventual eclipse of anarchism is not even posed, and from which therefore it would be completely incongruent to speak of resurgence.

Anarchy versus anarchism: a dubious dichotomy

The first scenario presents itself when *anarchy* is taken as the reference, more than anarchism, and it is defined as a certain *state of things* that would exist in the heart of this or that reality. A *state of things* whose defining characteristic would consist of excluding domination and where diversity and singularity could manifest themselves freely. "Anarchy" can be considered in fact as one of the possible multiple forms of reality. And it can be argued, for example, in a Bakuninist[9] tone, that biological life can only develop because it summons conditions for the free manifestation of diversity, of plurality, including the combination of contradictory elements; and because biological life is capable of smashing the constrictions that strive to repress its free expression and diversity. Thus, certain aspects of the living world call for a *state of anarchy* to be able to exist. In this sense, anarchy would be directly inscribed in life, as in other spheres of reality, which means that it would never totally disappear. Indeed it may be considered, in a gradualistic manner, that certain segments of reality carry with them *greater or lesser degrees of anarchy*.

It may be convenient to speak of anarchy as a certain state of things, as a form of reality that is accordingly intensely desirable for anarchists and towards which they would like to advance as quickly as possible. However, we can't cling to this reality on the basis of essentialist presuppositions, even though they would serve to exclude any possibility of an eventual disappearance of anarchy, guaranteeing that the latter could continue to exist, even when it manifests itself at a most basic level.

To think of anarchy as a really existing state of things does not exclude that this state of things be *contingent* rather than necessary, that it depends on variable circumstances that condition its existence, and that it can therefore suffer eclipses or even a definitive disappearance. Anarchy does not enjoy an existence *in itself*, but only exists on the basis of an activity, necessarily human, which constructs a specific conception of anarchy.

In effect, there is no "essence" of anarchism that exists beyond circumstance. Anarchy cannot be this or that *in itself*, but is the product of relations. It only acquires meaning in the context of a culture, of a

---

9 Mikhail Bakunin (1814–1876) was one of the earliest thinkers of modern anarchism, famously clashing with Karl Mark in the First International over the future of the working class movement. His activism, collectivist thought and links to propaganda of the deed were highly influential in the 19th century.

society and of a particular epoch. Its existence is defined by the context of domination it is resisting, experienced as such by the people who live in that context.

This means that, genealogically, for anarchy to exist and be understood as a differentiated and specific entity, not only must there exist apparatuses of domination and resistances to these apparatuses, but that furthermore, domination and resistance must be seen as a *possible experience* for subjects. Often domination is not understood as such, often it does not enter the field of the thinkable and often the resistances that it arouses are not experienced as such — in which case the conditions for the possibility of anarchy are not gathered together and anarchy, plainly, does not exist. For anarchy to exist it is necessary that, in addition to bringing together these conditions, certain ideas — such as, for example, those of singularity, freedom, autonomy and the struggle between domination and resistance — must be considered possible, something that does not happen until a certain period of historical development. Anarchy as a certain state of things, anarchy as an ontological entity, is not a pre-existent thing, it is a construction and, even, a relatively recent construction.

"Anarchy" and "anarchism" are, of course, two different phenomena, but the relation that they maintain reveals that they are intrinsically *connected*. Indeed, anarchy is meaningless except within the framework of *anarchist thought*. In other words, anarchy — understood in the specific way that anarchists give to the term — is a construction that reveals itself to be inseparable from anarchist thought, simply because it emerged from it. Furthermore, this thought is, for its part, but one of the constitutive elements of the *anarchist movement*, understanding by this a collection of practices, of discursive productions, of social and cultural events, of symbolic elements, etc., that form a specific historical fabric.

Therefore, to the extent that anarchy is a theoretical-practical production that emanates from the anarchist movement, it is not defined once and for all, but can vary with the eventual fluctuations of the anarchist movement and it can even disappear with this movement, because in the absence of the concept of anarchy, the movement would be totally undetectable in the heart of reality and its eventual existence would fall fully under the category of "unthinkable", or under that of simple historical vestige of what has only a past reality.

If I have dedicated so much space to the discussion of the concept of anarchy, it is in part because certain sectors of the anarchist movement, influenced, perhaps, by the thought of Hakim Bey[10] — to whom we will return later — currently give a decisive importance to this concept, which they oppose to that of anarchism. Anarchism would to them be the obscure side of anarchy, that would pervert and negate it in practice. In the face of this way of presenting things, it is necessary to see clearly that anarchy and anarchism are two completely inseparable elements, given that neither can exist without the other.

Anarchist movement and anarchist theory

The second scenario where an eventual collapse of anarchism would be meaningless presents itself when, having separated anarchism as a movement, on the one hand, and anarchism as theory, on the other, certain anarchist thinkers and propagandists, such as Peter Kropotkin[11], attribute to anarchism a millennial existence under the pretext that certain

---

10 Hakim Bey is best-known for *Temporary Autonomous Zone*, a 1991 book which described and helped popularise concepts around the creation of spaces beyond the reach of the ruling classes where social status quos are consciously challenged. Bey has been ostracised from anarchist circles since it emerged that he had been advocating for the "childlove movement", a pro-paedophilia grouping (see *Leaving Out the Ugly Part* by Robert Helms).

11 Freedom Press co-founder Peter Kropotkin (1842-1921) is popularly known as the founding philosopher of anarchist-communism. The former Russian prince, a polymath whose work on geography and biology was internationally renowned, renounced his title and was hugely influential in constructing the philosophical basis of modern anarchism through works such as *The Conquest of Bread*, *Mutual Aid* and his via many essays for journals including *Freedom*.

characteristic elements can already be found outlined or formulated since the most remote antiquity. It is clear that if such a perspective is adopted, it becomes difficult to speak of an eventual "collapse" of anarchism that would precede its current reappearance, given that it is always possible to discover conceptual traces of anarchism in a good many cultures, as far back as one goes in time.

If anarchism truly has accompanied us throughout the length of human history because it is inscribed, so to speak, in the human condition, the eventuality of its disappearance constitutes an aberration. Conversely, if we merge together in an inseparable whole *anarchism as a theoretical corpus and anarchism as a social movement*, this possibility becomes evident because anarchism requires, precisely, this theoretical corpus to exist.

What constitutes little by little anarchist thought and what establishes it as a distinct political tendency, from a certain moment and not before as "anarchism" is not separable from a social thought forged in the midst of very specific political, economic, cultural and social conditions, and of very definite social struggles. There is no anarchism without the development of capitalism; there is no anarchism without the analyses elaborated, for example, by Pierre Joseph Proudhon[12] regarding the social conditions created by the establishment of capitalism; and there is no anarchism without the struggles against exploitation carried out by workers, whether they be factory workers, artisans or peasants.

It is evident, therefore, that anarchism did not constitute itself, in Europe, as a definite political thought and, simultaneously, as a significant social movement, until the second half of the 19th century, *giving origin to, at the same time, to the anarchist concept of anarchy.* There is neither anarchism nor anarchy before then, however much certain precursors

---

12 Pierre Joseph Proudhon (1809-1865) was the first prominent intellectual to define himself in writing as an anarchist in the modern sense. The first mutualist, his seminal work *What is Property?* is often cited as marking the de facto birth of anarchism as a coherent philosophy.

anticipated some of its individual conceptual elements, however much social history may claim past demands and manifestations as its own, and however much, in the light of anarchism (once constituted as such), anarchistic inclinations can be observed in certain cultures as the current rise of anarchist anthropology makes clearly manifest.

Following on from this preliminary reflection on some theoretical scenarios rejecting the possibility of a disappearance, even momentary, of anarchy/anarchism, we are going to detain ourselves briefly with anarchism's history. I will not try to offer a full overview of such a rich and agitated history, which has already filled thousands of pages and which will continue to fill many thousands more. To dedicate to it, as I will here, only a few paragraphs, would be something of an affront to this history if I did not immediately indicate that my purpose is not to make known the history of anarchism — excellent books abound in this regard. Instead I will aim only to illustrate the reasons why anarchism eclipsed itself for a few decades.

Brief historical considerations

Among the principal references, we find, in the heat of the French Revolution of 1848, the writings of Joseph Déjacque, of Anselme Bellegarrigue[13] and, above all, of Pierre-Joseph Proudhon, who marked the beginnings of a political theory that identified itself as anarchist. Later, with the drive of industrialisation and the workers' movement (the creation of the International Workingmen's Association — IWA — in 1864), anarchist thought and the anarchist movement developed *simultaneously* through a series of struggles and events among which

---

13　Dejacque (1821-1865), a contemporary of Proudhon and active socialist militant, was the first known person to refer to himself in writing as a libertarian. Anselme Bellegarrigue was a participant in he French Revolution of 1848 and an individualist anarchist who edited multiple journals of the time.

stand out, undeniably, the Paris Commune of 1871[14] and the Saint Imier Congress of 1872[15]. The names of Mikhail Bakunin, of James Guillaume, of Peter Kropotkin, of Élisée Reclus, of Errico Malatesta, of Anselmo Lorenzo and of Ricardo Mella[16], among others, have remained closely associated with the growing relevance of a thought and of an activity that would place itself as a truly significant phenomenon and entity in the last decades of the 19th century and the first of the 20th century, culminating in the Spanish Revolution of 1936.

Anarchism was throughout those years a living thought; that is, a thought in continuous formation, evolving in osmosis with the social and cultural reality of the time, capable of enriching itself and modifying itself in contact with the world it exists within, through the experiences that it develops, thanks to the struggles in which it participates and the absorption of a part of the knowledge that circulates in its surroundings. The anarchist movement that feeds this thought, nourished itself in turn by it, is also capable of influencing reality, of producing certain effects within that will come to be notable in various European countries such as Spain, Italy, France, Germany, England, Russia or Ukraine, as well as in various Latin American countries—Argentina, Mexico and Brazil, among them—and, even, in the United States of America.

---

14 The Paris Commune marked a sea-change in thinking around both socialism and anarchism. The mass uprising, which unseated the French government and occupied the capital in 1871, was a touchstone for Marxists and anarchists alike and produced hugely important militants such as Louise Michel and Élisée Reclus.

15 The Saint Imier International was formed in 1872 following the expulsion of the anarchists from the First International. Lasting for seven years, it was the first explicit attempt to organise anarchists across Europe, taking a Bakuninist position.

16 James Guillaume (1844-1916) was heavily involved in the Jura Federation, primarily made up of Swiss watchmakers who were a key component of the anarchist wing of the First International, Errico Malatesta (1853-1932) was perhaps the single most influential anarchist thinker of the early 20th century, Anselmo Lorenzo (1841-1914) is often mentioned as the "grandfather" of Spanish anarchism, while Ricardo Mella (1861-1925) was an early advocate of anarchism in Galicia and a well-regarded anarchist theoretician.

Having demonstrated an appreciable vitality for about a century—*grosso modo* between 1860 and 1940, that is, some 80 years—anarchism fell back, inflected back upon itself and practically disappeared from the world political stage and from social struggles for several decades. It undertook a long journey in the wilderness that some writers took advantage of to stamp it with a certificate of dysfunctionality and to speak of it as of an *obsoles ideology* belonging to the past.

The fact is that, after the tragic defeat of the Spanish Revolution in 1939, if an exception is made for the libertarian presence in the anti-Franquista struggle, in the anti-fascist resistance in certain regions of Italy during World War II or in the active participation of British anarchists in the anti-nuclear campaigns of the end of the 1950s and the early 1960s or, also, a certain presence in Sweden and Argentina, for example, anarchism remained strikingly absent from the social struggles that marked the next 30 years in the many countries of the world. It was for the most part limited to a residual and testimonial role. Marginalised from struggles, unable to renew ties with social reality and relocate itself in political conflict, anarchism lost all possibility of re-actualising itself and of evolving.

In these unfavourable conditions, anarchism tended to fold in upon itself, becoming dogmatic, mummified, ruminating on its glorious past and developing powerful reflexes of self-preservation. The tendency towards a cult of memory over the will to renew led it, little by little, to become conservative, to defend its patrimony jealously and to close itself in a sterilising circle of mere repetition.

It is a little as if anarchism, in the absence of being practiced in the struggles against domination, had transformed itself slowly into the political equivalent of *a dead language*. That is, a language that, for lack of use by people, severs itself from the complex and changing reality in which it moved, becoming thereby sterile, incapable of evolving, of enriching itself, of being useful to apprehend and affect a moving reality.

A language which is not used is a relic rather than instrument; a fossil instead of a living body, a fixed image rather than a moving picture. As if it had been transformed into a dead language, anarchism fossilised itself from the beginnings of the 1940s until almost the end of the 1960s. This suspension of its vital functions occurred for a reason that I will not cease to insist upon and this is none other than the following: *anarchism is constantly forged in the practices of struggle against domination; outside of them, it withers away and decays.*

Stuck in the trance of stalled evolution, anarchism ceased to be properly anarchist and went on to become something else. There is no hidden mystery here, it is not a matter of alchemy, nor of the transmutation of bodies, but simply that if, as I maintain, what is proper to anarchism is rooted in being *constitutively changeable*, then the absence of change means simply that one is no longer dealing with anarchism.

The resurgence of anarchism

One has to wait until the end of the 1960s, with the large movements of opposition to the war in Vietnam, which saw incessant agitation on various university campuses across the United States, Germany, Italy and France, alongside the development, among a part of the youth, of nonconformist attitudes, sentiments of rebellion against authority and the challenge to social conventions and, finally, the fabulous explosion of May '68 in France, until a new stage in the flourishing of anarchism could begin.

Of course, even though strong libertarian tonalities resonated within it, May '68 was not anarchist. Yet it nevertheless inaugurated a new political radicality that harmonised with the stubborn obsession of anarchism to not reduce the struggle against the apparatuses of domination, the practices of exclusion or against the effects of stigmatisation and discrimination to the sole sphere of the economy and the relations of production.

What May '68 also inaugurated—even though it did not reach its full development until after the struggles in Seattle 1999[17]—was a form of anarchism that I call "anarchism outside its own walls" [*anarquismo extramuros*], because it developed unquestionably anarchist practices and values from outside specifically anarchist movements and at the margin of any explicit reference to anarchism.

May '68 finally announced, in the very heart of militant anarchism, novel conceptions that, as Todd May[18] says, privileged (among other things) tactical perspectives before strategic orientations, outlining thereby a new libertarian *ethos*. In effect, actions undertaken with the aim of developing political organisations and projects that had as an objective and as a horizon the global transformation of society gave way to actions destined at directly subverting the existing concrete and limited aspects of instituted society.

Some 30 years after May '68, large demonstrations for a different kind of globalisation [*altermundista*] in the early 2000s allowed anarchism to experience a new growth and acquire, thanks to a strong presence in struggles and in the streets, a spectacular projection. The use of the internet allows for the rapid communication of anarchist protests of all kinds as they take place in the most diverse parts of the world; it permits assuring an immediate and almost exhaustive coverage of these events; it is also no less certain that no single day goes by without different anarchist portals announcing one or even several libertarian events. Without letting ourselves be dazzled by the multiplying effect that the internet produces, it has to be acknowledged that the proliferation of libertarian activities in the beginning of this century was hard to imagine just a few years ago.

---

17 The Seattle World Trade Organisation counter-protests of 1999 kicked off a series of major confrontations where anti-capitalists attempted to make it impossible for world leaders to hold gatherings in major cities. The scale and militancy of the protests, which comprehensively wrong-footed police, were heralded as a seachange in the reach and mobilisation capacities of the anti-globalisation movement.

18 One of the fathers of postanarchism, see page 60.

This upsurge of anarchism not only showed itself in struggles and in the streets, but extended also to the sphere of culture and, even, to the domain of the university as, for example, in the creation in October of 2005, at the English university of Loughborough, of a dense academic network of reflection and exchange called the *Anarchist Studies Network*, followed by the creation in 2009 of *North American Anarchist Studies*. Or as is made evident by the constitution of an ample international network that brings together an impressive number of university researchers who define themselves as anarchists or who are interested in anarchism. The colloquia dedicated to different aspects of anarchism — historical, political, philosophical — continue to multiply (Paris, Lyon, Rio de Janeiro, Mexico among others).

This abundant presence of anarchism in the world of academia cannot but astound us, those who had the experience of its absolute non-existence within the institutions, during the long winter that Marxist hegemony represented, which followed conservative hegemony, or coexisted with it, above all in countries like France and Italy. In truth, the panorama outlined above would have been unimaginable even a few years ago, even as recently as the end of the 1990s.

Let us point out, finally, that between May '68 and the protests of the 2000s, anarchism demonstrated an upsurge of vitality on various occasions, above all in Spain. In the years 1976-1978, the extraordinary libertarian effervescence that followed the death of Franco left us completely stupefied, all the more stupefied the more closely we were tied to the fragile reality of Spanish anarchism in the last years of *Franquismo*. An effervescence that was capable of gathering in 1977 some 100,000 participants during a meeting of the CNT in Barcelona and that allowed that same year the coming together of thousands of anarchists from across the globe to participate in the *Jornadas Libertarias* in this same city. A vitality that showed itself also in Venice, in September 1984, where thousands of anarchists gathered, coming from everywhere, and in the large international gathering celebrated in Barcelona in September-October of 1993.

After the explosion of the events of May '68, anarchists regularly gathered around events in numbers previously unimaginable. In fact, the resurgence of anarchism has not ceased to make us jump, so to speak, from surprise to surprise. May '68 was a surprise for everyone, including of course the few anarchists who were wandering the streets of Paris, a little before. Spain immediately after Franco was another surprise, above all for the few anarchists who had continued to struggle during the last years of the dictatorship. The anarchist effervescence of the 2000s is, finally, a third surprise that has no need to envy those that preceded it.

How will, then, the fourth surprise be that the immediate future undoubtedly holds out for us?

THE FORM THAT THE RESURGENCE OF
ANARCHISM TAKES: NEOANARCHISM

Translators' note: Ibáñez, not without hesitation and only as a heuristic, employs the term "neoanarchism" to refer to the resurgence and changing nature of the movement in the wake of May 1968, France. But these changes have not been without their critics. Here he endeavours to both explain and defend what he considers to be the virtues of our new anarchism.

It is very obvious that the kind of anarchism that was slowly created after May '68, and which gained a sudden boost in the beginning of the 2000s, marked a seachange. To paraphrase the poet Paul Verlaine, one could say that it was no longer *"ni tout à fait le même ni tout à fait un autre"* [*neither completely the same nor completely different*]. It was a somewhat different form of anarchism which generated itself in and through some practices of struggle against domination that began to extend itself towards the end of the 1960s, following in the wake of the events of May '68.

It seems particularly clear that if anarchism regained protagonism, it has been, above all, because the changes that have occurred at various levels of social, cultural, political and technological reality have created conditions today which resonate with some of the characteristics of anarchism. This consonance explains how contemporary anarchism responds far better than other currents of socially engaged political thought to the particularities and the *exigencies of the present*.

Nevertheless, if this harmony between certain features of anarchism and certain characteristics of the current epoch have permitted its expansion, such that anarchism reveals itself as a well adapted instrument to the struggles and the conditions of the present, it has also had a retroactive bearing on some of its features. Indeed, these features have been modified as a consequence of the involvement of anarchism in today's society and as a *return effect* on its very capacity to have an impact on reality.

We have then, on the one hand, the constitution of a new reality that is peculiarly amenable towards anarchist intervention and, on the other hand, an anarchism that renews itself precisely because of its action on that reality. It is from this double process or, stated differently, from this *coupling* between reality and anarchism, that the latter has again become truly contemporaneous, meaning that anarchism finds itself *in consonance* with the demands of struggles provoked in the present day.

Even knowing full well that no such current exists, that there is neither a doctrine nor an identity that presently calls itself *neoanarchist* and that to promote a new adjective for anarchism — one more — is of little interest, I resort to this expression as a convenient and provisional way to designate this somewhat different anarchism that we find in the beginning of this century.

Anarchism outside its own walls

If there is something that powerfully calls our attention when we observe contemporary anarchism, it is, without any doubt, *its significant expansion beyond the frontiers of the anarchist movement*. It is true that anarchism has always overflown the contours, ultimately considerably confused, of the self-defining movement, but this overflowing has been amplified in a spectacular fashion since May '68 until the most recent protest movements, with their massive occupations of public squares and streets (Seattle, the 15M movement[19], Occupy Wall Street[20], etc.).

This expansion of anarchism outside its borders is not only of a greater dimension than in the past, it also presents somewhat different features. In effect, it is no longer a matter of an essentially cultural type of overflow, as when some artists, certain singer-songwriters and a few intellectuals sometimes expressed their proximity to libertarian ideas. Today the overflow manifests itself in the very heart of specific struggles undertaken by opposition movements that make no direct claim to anarchism.

Firstly, in the final stages of May '68, we witnessed the creation of *new social movements* that struggled, on "identitarian" bases, for the recognition of certain categories of people that were strongly discriminated against and stigmatised. These movements were not anarchist, far from it, but on some matters, they moved close to it. In any case, they moved away from classical political schemas, far more *centralised* in their forms of organisation and struggle, as well as showing themselves to be *much less sensitive to the problematic of relations of power*. It was in this way that struggles against various types of domination gained, little by little, a certain importance alongside more traditional struggles anchored in the economic sphere and the world of work.

Subsequently, towards the end of the 1990s, a new inflection occurred with the appearance of the alter-globalisation movement, a *movement of movements*. Despite its enormous heterogeneity and despite all of the criticism that can be directed at it, it is a movement that bears strong libertarian resonances. It is made up, basically, as everyone knows

---

19 15M, also known as the Indignados movement, was a hugely successful four-year campaign against austerity in Spain. Containing broad anarchist influences, it mobilised tens of thousands of people, helped popularise forms of direct action and forced a significant realignment of the political landscape.

20 Taking place a few months after 15M began, Occupy Wall Street was for a time a globally-recognised resistance space which took over the heart of the world's financial headquarters. It inspired similar actions across the US and worldwide.

today, of collectives and people active outside specifically anarchist organisations, but who encounter or who reinvent, in struggles, anti-hierarchical, anti-centralist and anti-representative political forms that are quite close to anarchism, as much with regards to decision-making methods, as to forms of organisation and the modalities that characterise their actions; actions that in fact often make theirs principles of direct action.

A good number of the activists associated with the movement of movements/alter-globalisation movement — not all, of course — show themselves to be more fiercely committed to the defence of certain anti-authoritarian practices than some so-called anarchists. At times, it even occurs that they demonstrate themselves to be more intransigent than the anarchists in the demand that the characteristics of actions undertaken, as well as modes of decision making and forms of organisation adopted, be truly *prefigurative*. That is, they reflect in their very characteristics the goals sought.

Finally, at the beginning of the second decade of this century, massive occupations of public spaces in Spain's cities occurred, followed by those of Wall Street in New York and in other cities of the United States and across Europe, which also adopted forms of organisation and modes of action with a close affinity to anarchist practices.

The novelty therefore is that today the anarchist movement is no longer *the only depositary*, the only defender of certain anti-hierarchical principles, nor of certain non-authoritarian practices, nor of horizontal forms of organisation, nor of the capacity to undertake struggles that present libertarian tonalities, nor of *mistrust towards all apparatuses of power, whatever they may be*. These elements *have spread beyond the anarchist movement*, and are taken up today by collectives that do not identify themselves with the anarchist label and that sometimes even make explicit their refusal to allow themselves to be closed within the folds of this identity.

To avoid possible misunderstandings, it is important to clarify that this is not a matter of enlisting, under the flag of anarchism, movements that make no reference to it and of qualifying as anarchist any popular demonstration basing itself on direct democracy. Neither the great protest of Seattle, nor the 15M movement, nor Occupy Wall Street were explicitly anarchist, and their subsequent shifts can even end up contradicting their initial libertarian tonalities. Anarchism does not only consist of certain formal organisational modalities, but is also based on substantive ideas that are fundamental to define it. In fact, the paradox could occur of certain social movements adopting anarchist organisational models to promote authoritarian political notions. It is obvious that horizontal and assembly-based functioning is not sufficient to be able to speak of anarchist practices.

However, it is undeniable that the movements that I have referred to have a "family resemblance" to anarchism, placing them clearly in its ideological field and that these demonstrations form part of an *anarchism in action*, even if they do not claim the name for themselves and even if they effect changes in its traditional forms. It is in part to designate this somewhat diffuse, non-identitarian, form of anarchism, forged directly in contemporary struggles and *outside the anarchist movement* that I have recourse to use the expression "anarchism outside its own walls" [*anarquismo extramurros*]. Curiously, this kind of anarchism also includes, at least in Spain, people who defined themselves as anarchists, but who renounced the label so as to be closer and more involved in the kinds of globally libertarian practices and sensitivities that characterise some of the new rebellious movements.

The new activist fabric and the anarchist identity

Non-identitarian anarchism is part of neoanarchism, though it represents only one of its aspects, one of its facets. The other face of neoanarchism is comprised of collectives and people—generally very young—who even though they affirm themselves as explicitly anarchist, they nevertheless express a new sensibility with respect to this identitarian ascription. Their way of assuming an anarchist identity is marked by a flexibility and an openness which articulate a different relation with the anarchist tradition on the one hand, and with opposition movements outside this tradition, on the other. The borders between these two realities in fact become more permeable, more porous, dependence on the anarchist tradition becomes more flexible and, above all, this tradition is understood as having to be cultivated, enriched and, therefore, transformed and reformulated by inclusions and, even, by a *hybridisation*, by a certain *blending* [*mestizaje*], with contributions coming from struggles framed within other traditions.

It is not a matter of incorporating into anarchism a few elements of external political thought. It concerns rather, and above all, *producing together*, with other collectives also committed to struggles against domination, elements that are incorporated within the anarchist tradition, making it move. This openness of neoanarchism could be illustrated in that famous phrase which states, more or less, the following: "Alone we cannot, but, in addition, it would be pointless". It is this same sensibility that we find in the declaration of the *Planetary Alternatives Network* (PAN[21]), where one can read:

"We are, however, profoundly anti-sectarian, by which we mean two things. We do not attempt to enforce any particular form of anarchism on one another [...] We value diversity as a principle in itself, limited only by our common rejection of structures of domination. Since we see anarchism not as a doctrine so much as a process of movement towards a free, just, and sustainable, society, we believe anarchists should not limit themselves to cooperating

---

21 The Planetary Alternatives Network was a shortlived attempt in 2003 to build an anti-globalisation international based on anarchist principles. The "hallmarks" of the intended group can be found at ainfos.ca/03/oct/ainfos00520.html

with those who self-identify as anarchists, but should actively seek to cooperate with anyone who is working to create a world based on those same broad liberatory principles, and, in fact, to learn from them. One of the purposes of the International is to facilitate this: both to make it easier for us to bring some of those millions around the world who are, effectively, anarchists without knowing it, into touch with the thoughts of others who have worked in that same tradition, and, at the same time, to enrich the anarchist tradition itself through contact with their experiences."

This redefinition has important repercussions on *the anarchist imaginary* and this is significant because, as we well know, it is not generally due to prior knowledge of theoretical texts that young people approach the anarchist movement. It is not by virtue of the writings of Proudhon or Bakunin that there are those who adhere, but because of a particular imaginary; and it is not until later that the canonical texts are eventually read.

The anarchist imaginary has in fact never ceased to enrich itself, integrating, among other things, the great historical episodes of struggle against domination, as manifested in different parts of the world. What it has made its own over the last few years has been, for example, the barricades, the occupations and the slogans of May '68 and, after 1986, a series of phenomena such as the anarcho-punk scene (that developed with force starting in the 1980s and which was an authentic breeding ground for young anarchists) and the occupation movement, with its unique aesthetic and lifestyle. These are some of the elements that have continued to nourish and spur on this imaginary.

It has however undoubtedly been the great international episodes of struggles against various forms of domination (that, without wanting to be exhaustive, go from Chiapas in 1994 to Taksim Square in 2013, passing through Seattle in 1999, Quebec, Gothenburg and Genova in 2001, the *No Borders* camp in Strasbourg in 2002, the Athens neighbourhood of

Exarchia uninterruptedly since 2008 and Madrid, Barcelona or New York in 2011) that have revitalised the current anarchist imaginary. This imaginary, a little different from that of the earlier period, which generally began with the Paris Commune, moving through the Chicago Martyrs and the misnamed Tragic Week of Barcelona, on to the mutinous sailors of Kronstadt and the *Maknovtchina* of Ukraine, finishing in the Spanish Revolution, is that which today provokes identitarian adherence among anarchist youth. It seems obvious that the new elements which constitute it inevitably redraw the outlines of this identity.

In brief, the contemporary anarchist identity is not at all the same as the old one. It cannot be the same because what constitutes its imaginary sustains itself also from struggles developed by current protest movements, and these present features different from older struggles.

These new forms of struggle do not appear by chance and they are not the result of a new political strategy deliberately elaborated somewhere. They are rather the direct result of a recomposition and renewal of the apparatuses and modalities of domination that accompany the social changes of the last few decades. *The practices of struggle against domination are changing at the same time as the forms of domination change*; and this is absolutely normal because struggles are always provoked by and defined *by that against which they constitute themselves*. It is the new forms of domination which have appeared in our societies that give rise to current resistances and the structure they possess.

The configuration of society in a network, the path from the pyramidal to the reticular and the horizontal, the deployment of new information and communication technologies (or "NICTs"), all evidently put into movement new forms of domination. It also however facilitates the development of extraordinarily effective practices of subversion which happen to reflect the organisational forms proper to anarchism.

It is the forms adapted by the practices of struggle against the current forms of domination and, more specifically, those that are developed by the new movements of opposition, which find themselves incorporated, partly, in contemporary anarchism and which serve to outline a neoanarchism.

As long as it finds itself in direct connection with these struggles, neoanarchism shares in their imaginary and joins their principle characteristics with an anarchist imaginary which cannot but be modified.

The current revolutionary imaginary

One of the most striking features of this modification concerns the revolutionary imaginary itself.

The stimulus and incitement value that generalised insurrection might provide in a classical revolutionary imaginary is effectively replaced in a neoanarchist imaginary by an attraction to what could be called *the continuous and immediate revolution*. That is, revolution comes to be considered a *constitutive* dimension of subversive action itself. Revolution is conceived of as something that is anchored in the present and that it is not therefore something that is only desired and dreamed of as a future event, but is *essentially lived*.

The revolutionary is the will to break the apparatuses of concrete and situated domination, it is the effort to block power in its multiple manifestations, and it is action taken to create spaces that are radically separate from the values and the modes of life induced by capitalism. An emphasis is thus placed *on the present* and on *its transformation, limited but radical,* and it is therefore for this reason that so many efforts are dedicated to creating spaces of life and forms of being that are situated in radical rupture with the norms of the system and which give rise to new rebellious subjectivities.

It can indeed be seen clearly today that the old revolutionary imaginary conveyed the hope of a possible dominion of society as a whole, and that this hope was the bearer of inevitable totalitarian deviations that were translated into actions, in the case of politics referenced to Marxism, and that remained only in outline, though still perceptible, in those inspired by anarchism.

Likewise, beneath the standard of universalism which could be nothing other than — as with all universalisms — a masked particularism, this imaginary concealed a will to dissolve differences within the framework of a project that, claiming to be *valid for everyone*, negated in practice the legitimate pluralism of political options and values. Finally, the messianic stink of an *eschatology* that strove to subordinate life to the promise of living, and to justify all sufferings and renunciations in the name of an abstraction, was so profoundly encrusted in this imaginary that it blocked the exercise of any trace of critical thought.

Nowadays, the explicit rejection of our iniquitous social conditions of existence remains intact, as well as the desire to illuminate radically different conditions. Nevertheless, the concept of *revolution* is profoundly redefined from a fully presentist perspective. The idea of *a radical rupture* continues to be held, but without any eschatological point of view. On the contrary, nothing can be proposed for the day after the revolution, *because it cannot be located in the future.* Its only home is the present and *it is produced in each space and in each instant that it is possible to withdraw oneself from the system.*

What is new in the present is that the will of radical rupture can appeal to nothing more than the negation of obedience, to rebelliousness and to profound disagreement with established reality. No object of substitution is necessary to reject what is imposed upon us; no *progress towards ...* no *advance in the direction of ...* are required to measure the reach of the consequences of a struggle. The measuring rod with which the new antagonists evaluate the compass of their struggles is not exterior to them and is in no way guided by the more or less wide path that struggles have been allowed to use to approach an objective that would exceed the situated, limited, concrete and particular character of the same.

This is, for example, what one comes away with from a text by the US collective CrimethInc:

Our revolution must be immediate *revolution in our daily lives …* *[We] must seek first and foremost to alter the contents of our own lives in a revolutionary manner, rather than direct our struggle towards world-historical changes which we will not live to witness.* (Days of War, Nights of Love)

It seems clearly evident that the new struggles contribute especially to the multiplication and dissemination of centres of resistance against very concrete and distinctly situated injustices, impositions and discriminations. It is perhaps this dissemination that explains the great diversity that today characterises a movement fragmented into a multiplicity of currents running from green anarchism to insurrectionism, from anarcho-feminists to the anarcho-punk movement, from anti-speciesism and veganism to the self-named organised anarchism — generally, of the communist libertarian variety — without forgetting that anarcho-syndicalism continues to have strong roots in a country like Spain, where it counts on two principal organisations that represent, *grosso modo*, the two traditional currents of Spanish anarcho-syndicalism.[22]

Either way, it is not only that the perspective of a global transformation giving birth to a new society no longer constitutes the nerve that today dynamises and orients struggles. It is moreover that the struggles which aspire to be global or *totalising* inspire, rather, a certain mistrust because they are seen as tending to reproduce, sooner or later, that which they purport to combat. If in fact capitalism and the apparatuses of domination

---

22 The CNT (see note, page vi) and the CGT. The latter is the larger of the two organisations and was initially formed from a split with the CNT over whether workers should participate in works councils, though more truly distinct ideological perspectives have since emerged.

need, imperatively, to affect *the totality of society*, it is because they can only function in a context where no single fragment has the possibility of escaping its control. Conversely, the resistances would fatally separate themselves from their reason for being if they intended to remake society in its totality and in all of its aspects. It is a matter then of attacking the local establishment and manifestations of domination, renouncing a confrontation on a more general level, something that would call upon resources of a similar power and nature to those used by the very system to control the ensemble of society.

For this reason, even though the effort to regroup as many forces and wills as is possible continues, the construction of large organisations, solidly structured and anchored in a specific territory, can no longer be found on the majority of current subversive agendas. On the contrary, what is seen is a preservation of the fluidity of the networks that are created and the avoidance of crystallisation into excessively strong organisations, which only present the appearance of efficiency and which end in sterilising struggles. This fluidity is especially emphasised in the insurrectionalist position, inspired at its origin by the Italian anarchist Alfredo Bonanno[23], but which, since then, has evolved and diversified itself. Let us recall that insurrectionists advocate four major tactics:

1. Desertion — *exodus* — consisting of escaping the places where practices of hierarchical domination exist;
2. Sabotage;
3. Occupation of spaces — streets, places, official buildings, etc.
4. The articulation of two kinds of spaces, later codified by Hakim Bey: Temporary Autonomous Zones (TAZ) and Permanent Autonomous Zones (PAZ).

---

23 Alfredo Bonanno is a Sicilian insurrectionist and author of *Armed Joy* among other works.

While they virulently criticise classical anarchist organisations, proposing much more lax, fluid and informal organisational structures and privileging the creation of small autonomous groups based on relations of affinity, the insurrectionists continue to defend an idea of revolution that has certain resonances with the traditional.

The construction of the present and constructive anarchism

The emphasis contemporary anarchism places on transforming the present and redefining revolution as a reality that does not await us at the end of a path of struggle, but as something occurring within struggles themselves and the forms of life that they give rise to, relates to its present day success.

Indeed, to remain coherent in its focus on the present, anarchism sees itself committed to offering, *concrete realisations* which make it possible to live now, even though only partially, in another society, to weave other social relations and develop another mode of life. These realisations go from self-managed spaces to networks of exchange and mutual aid, moving through occupied spaces to all kinds of cooperatives.

It is basically with concrete achievements rather than cheques to be cashed in the future that the promises of the revolution are paid, and they intensely seduce a selection of those who reject current society. It is therefore also because anarchism offers an ensemble of concrete realisations transforming the present and which permit changing oneself, that it today enjoys an undeniable success among certain groups of youth.

To struggle no longer consists only of denouncing, opposing and confronting, it is also to *create, here and now, different realities*. Struggles have to produce concrete results without ceasing to be conditioned by hopes placed in the future. To learn how to struggle without illusions with regards to the future leads us to judge the value of a struggle on its own merit. It is in the very reality of struggles, in their concrete results and specific approaches that the whole of their value lies, and this must not be sought in what is to be found beyond them — for example, in this or that final objective that would give them "legitimacy".

It is consequently about tearing spaces away from the system, developing community experiences that have a transformative character. Because it's only when an activity truly and radically transforms a reality — even if only provisionally and partially — that it establishes the basis for going beyond a mere — though always necessary — opposition to the system, creating a concrete alternative. This is an approach that Proudhon had previously advocated when he questioned the virtues of destruction and of opposition, and when he emphasised the construction of alternatives. It is also what Colin Ward[24] defended in the 1970s when, anticipating certain neoanarchist positions, he said that anarchism, far from being negation, was the construction here and now of alternatives that abide by principles other than those of domination. It is lastly what Gustav Landauer proclaimed in the beginning of the last century when he wrote this phrase that I mentioned in the preamble: "Anarchism is not a thing of the future but of the present: it is not a question of demands but of life".

It is accordingly necessary to act upon a milieu that we transform, which in turn allows us to transform ourselves, modifying our subjectivity. This is possible by creating different social ties, constructing complicities and relations of solidarity which outline, in practice and in the present, a different reality and another life. As stated in the French journal *Tiqqun*[25]: "It is a matter of establishing modes of life that are in themselves modes of struggle". Of course, none of this is completely new and it can be related,

---

24 One of the most influential English anarchists of modern times, Colin Ward was a major figure at Freedom Press, editing *Anarchy* magazine, helping edit *Freedom* newspaper and authoring multiple major works including *Anarchy in Action*.
25 While it only ran for two issues in 1999, *Tiqqun* has been influential in the autonomist and squatter communities with its poetic and semi-insurrectionary approach.

in part, to the *lieux de vie*—places of life—created by individualist anarchists towards the end of the 19th century and the beginning of the 20th.

The criticisms of these approaches also began long ago. It is indeed clear that the system cannot tolerate an *outside* with respect to itself and cannot accept that certain fragments of society escape its control. It would therefore be absurd to think that *spaces outside the system* can proliferate to the point of being able to progressively subvert and dismantle it. The little islands of freedom are a danger and the system draws its claws well before a threat can grow. This marks the limits of the pretensions to change society by means of the creation of *another society* in the midst of that which already exists.

This realisation certainly invalidates any excessive confidence placed in the constructive dimension of anarchism, but it does not diminish its interest. The system cannot permanently control everything, and struggles are possible because they encounter and open spaces that escape, in part and during some time, the strict control of that system. So too the spaces removed from the system via the concrete realisations of anarchism can subsist for a more or less prolonged period of time.

This is important because, as we well know, besides oppressing, repressing and crushing human beings, the apparatuses and practices of domination always constitute *modes of subjectification* of individuals. They mould their imaginary, their desires and their way of thinking such that they respond, freely and spontaneously, in a way that the dominant authorities expect. It is for this reason that we cannot change our desires if we do not change the form of life that produces them—thus the importance of creating forms of life and spaces that permit *de-subjectificiation*. It is ultimately an issue, today as in the past, of producing a political subjectivity that is radically rebellious against existing society, to the commodity values that constitute it and the relations of exploitation and domination that ground it.

It is not uncommon to hear neoanarchists say, with strong Foucaldian accents, that it is a matter of transforming oneself, of changing our current subjectivity, of *inventing ourselves outside of the matrix that has formed us.* But, notice, this does not refer to a purely individual practice, because it is obviously in relation to others, in the fabric of relations, in collective practices and common struggles, where materials and tools are found to carry out this labour upon oneself.

Coincidentally, the importance that practices of de-subjectification have achieved today directly confront the famous dichotomy that Murray Bookchin established, in the mid-1990s, between *social anarchism* and *lifestyle anarchism*, because both kinds of anarchism, far from being opposed to each other, are intimately connected. The necessary construction of a different subjectivity through struggles, whether with a local or global perspective, implies in effect that there is no *social anarchism* that does not involve strong existential elements — and that *lifestyle anarchism* does not exist without social aspects.

It is often said that, contrary to what occurs with rebellions rooted in the social question, that rebellions qualified as *existential* are totally innocuous for the system because, even though they may overflow the strictly private sphere, they remain confined to reduced spaces which are unable to perturb the proper functioning of that system.

Things are not however like this. If anarchism, which is also — above all, some would say — a way of being, a mode of living and of feeling, a form of sensitivity and, therefore, a clearly existential option, represents a problem for the system, it is because in part it strongly resists not only the status quo's intimidations, but, above all, its manoeuvres of seduction and integration. With evident exceptions, it is in fact quite frequent that those profoundly marked by their anarchist experience remain *irrecoverable.* In keeping alive their irreducible alterity with respect to the system, they obviously represent a danger to it. It is not that they permanently challenge it by their mere existence, but that they also serve as relays so that new rebellious sensitivities are born. This sustains a certain relation with something that Christian Ferrer[26], a good friend and anarchist philosopher, used to say to me: "Anarchism is not taught and nor is it learned in books — though these may help — but is spread by contagion; and when someone is infected, more often than not, it is forever".

I believe then that *social (*or *organised) anarchism* and *lifestyle anarchism* mutually imply each other. Certainly to the degree that, on one hand, the challenge represented by adopting a lifestyle different from that of the established system and refusing to abide by its norms and values constitutes a form of struggle which corrodes its pretension to ideological hegemony and which gives rise to social conflict, when the system takes normalising measures or when dissidents develop activities of harassment. In either case, lifestyle anarchism produces effects of social change that may sometimes be notable.

On the other hand, it is obvious that no-one can fight for collective emancipation and commit themselves to social struggles without it profoundly affecting their lifestyle and way of being. It turns out, in addition, that the two forms of anarchism frequently coincide on the terrain of concrete struggles. This does impede certain determined elements of the anarchist movement from raising barriers between these two ways of practicing anarchism. It is because I am convinced that these barriers weaken anarchism, that I would like to argue briefly here against those who try and consolidate them.

In general, those who are catalogued, in the majority of cases against their will, as supporters of lifestyle anarchism — among whom would be included the majority of neoanarchists — show themselves to be relaxed about the differentiation between libertarian ideological currents and show little interest in internal movement struggle. It is more often those

---

26 Ferrer is an Argentinian sociologist and essayist at the University of Buenos Aires. Key themes in his work include technology and society, the philosophy of anarchism, networks of power, freedom, and social control.

who are in favour of social or organised anarchism — overlapping, in good measure, with libertarian communist positions — who strive to extend their sphere of influence in the heart of the movement and confine "lifestyle" anarchists to its margins. It is therefore their arguments that I would like to discuss here, but not without first spelling out certain points, to avoid misunderstandings.

It is obvious that an anarchism "without adjectives" is only sustainable as anarchism if it is committed to social justice and freedom among equals. Not only must it denounce exploitation and social inequalities, it must also struggle against them in the most efficacious way possible. It must be present among those who have committed themselves in these struggles and must endeavour to expand its influence among those most directly affected by the injustices of the system. There is nothing to be said consequently against the efforts that certain anarchists deploy to organise themselves with the aim of contributing to better develop those struggles. Nevertheless, it is also obvious that social or organised anarchism conveys, with excessive frequency, practices and political assumptions that surreptitiously distance it from its libertarian roots. Either because it adopts insufficiently horizontal structures — if not on paper, in practice — or because it lets itself be tempted by a certain vanguardism, or because it is inclined to develop sectarian practices, among other things.

Capitalism is of course our most direct enemy and it should not be given any respite. The struggle against it constitutes an unrenounceable need for anarchism. However, considering the diversity that characterises the more than seven billion human beings who inhabit the planet, it is unreasonable to think that our values and social models can succeed in bringing together the preferences of the majority. *Totalizing* perspectives are of no value to us, therefore, neither within the frame of the vast "global world", nor in the frame of a particular society. If we do not wish to resuscitate utopian illusions, we must accept that, for those of us who are committed to battles in favour of emancipation, that we will never know final success, nor the advent of the kind of society that we dream of. All we can know is the experience of these struggles and their (never definitive) results. Consequently, social anarchism or not, organised anarchism or not, in the last instance, we have to wager on *the modification of the present*—a necessarily local and partial modification—turning a deaf ear to the songs of the totalising sirens and abandoning illusions of an endpoint.

If it is not possible to establish a generalised libertarian communism, nor to render anarchist the whole of the human population, or even a particular society, what can anarchism aspire to and what is left?

Well, even so, what remains is the ongoing struggle against domination in its multiple facets and this includes, of course, domination in the economic sphere, even though it goes well beyond this. What also remains is the transformation of the present, always localised and partial, but radical, and this includes our own transformation. And finally, we have to escape from our confinement and our ghetto, to act together with others, not to convince them, but to accept them. Not for strategic reasons, but for reasons of *principle*.

To act with others? You are right comrades, those of you who struggle in the heart of "organised" anarchism. To act with others as you often do is honourable, however it also means to act with anarchists who do not enlist under the flag of organisations laying claim to "social anarchism", but who, far from finding refuge in the private sphere, are also committed to radical struggles. As indeed usually happens with dualisms, the dichotomy suggested by Bookchin deforms reality because there are not *two categories* of anarchism, but a single *continuous one*. At one extreme, we find a lifestyle anarchism withdrawn into itself and totally indifferent to social struggles, while at the other extreme, one finds a social anarchism impermeable to everything other than the social struggle against capital. Between these two extremes, unfolds an array where all of the doses between the two types of anarchism are represented.

What creates the dichotomy, leaving as it does only two possibilities open, is the eventuality of *belonging or not* to a specific organisation. But if the dichotomy originates in this fact, then it is obvious that it cannot serve to say that "social anarchism" is to be found on one side and that what is found on the other side is not social.

The same comment can be applied to the expression "organised anarchism". There is not *an* organised anarchism, on the one hand, and another which is not, on the other hand. It is obvious that one has to organise oneself and that the development of any type of collective activity always calls for some form of organisation and organised activity, even if only to publish a few pages or to debate an issue. Therefore, the question is not whether to organise oneself, but *how*. And the answer is that to know how to organise ourselves, we have to know *for what purpose we want to organise*. This conditions the form of organisation.

A traditional model presupposes the creation of a permanent, stable and encompassing organisational structure, articulated around a few programmatic bases and with some common long-term objectives. It is a model that got on poorly with actual social conditions and that lost a considerable part of its effectiveness in times of rapid change. Today's reality demands much more flexible, more fluid, models, guided by simple aims of *coordination* to carry out concrete and specific tasks. Such forms of organisation must necessarily adjust quickly to the nature of the tasks and the objectives for which they were created, and as they take diverse, variable, and transitory forms, a multiplicity of organisational forms must also co-exist in as complementary a way as possible, without doubting that they can disappear or transform according to the rhythm of social changes and events.

The question of organisation should probably be rethought and given new meaning in the same way as occurred with the concept of revolution, not to proclaim the absence or uselessness of organisation, but to renew its conceptualisation, its forms and practices. It's clear that the fascination currently exercised, in certain activist circles, by older models of organisation—brandished as a panacea to increase the effectiveness and diffusion of anarchism—in no way facilitates this task. The efforts dedicated to the construction of an anarchist organisation and the priority given to this labour diverts attention away from tasks more directly tied to struggles, sustaining the illusion that the difficulties that trouble current struggles are due principally to the absence of a grande libertarian organisation and that these will disappear as soon as the latter sees the light of day.

The preoccupation with organising and organisational activity must be constant in order to develop collective activities. However, this is very different from the determination *to construct an organisation*. For this reason, the use of the expression "organised anarchism" is deceptive. It is an expression that basically refers to anarchism framed as a classical type of organisation bound to the insistent effort to construct such an organisation and suggests that, no matter how organised certain anarchist groups or collectives are for carrying out concrete and specific tasks, they form no part of it.

The expression is deceitful, but also dangerous because it introduces, as almost all dichotomies do, an asymmetry of value and *a hierarchisation*. Accordingly, given that the fact of organising oneself constitutes, obviously, a positive value, organised anarchism is regarded as valid and the other type of anarchism is contemptible. Evidently, the difference between them does not reside in being organised or not, *both are*, but because one is marked by a specific organisation or aims to construct it and the other is not. But of course, if things were said in this manner, the phrase "organised anarchism" would lose much of its mystique and calls to construct "the organisation" would be weakened.

My way of dealing with this question should not be interpreted as an argument for an anarchism closed within the sphere of the individual. To question the dichotomy created by separating social anarchism and organised anarchism does not mean that anarchism should not achieve *a social projection* and, more precisely, *a projection within social movements*. If anarchism has revived in the present, it is precisely because it has been present in the large popular mobilisations of the beginning of this century. And it is obvious that if anarchism wants to have any kind of validity, it must pervade the broadest social movements possible—as Spanish anarchism did until the end of the 1930s. This implies of course that these movements cannot be composed principally of anarchists, nor must they be specifically anarchist. This libertarian impregnation, through the presence of anarchist militants, as well as people and collectives that *act in a libertarian manner*, even though they do not define themselves as such, can be observed more recently in the multitudinous mobilisations that do not cease to amplify and radicalise themselves in France, from 2008 until today, against the construction of an airport in Notre-Dame-des-Landes, in Brittany[27], or the mobilisations against evictions in Spain.

If contemporary anarchism changes, it is precisely because it finds itself involved, *with other collectives*, in current struggles and because it incorporates into itself the principal characteristics of these struggles. Because it finds itself in harmony with these struggles, neoanarchism participates in their imaginary and gathers into itself some of their features in an anarchist imaginary which cannot therefore but see itself modified. Ultimately, the anarchism that changes is *the anarchism that struggles* in *the present*.

As I already indicated, "neoanarchism" appears to be the easiest way to indicate changes experienced by a significant part of contemporary anarchists. This expression though can also conceal certain *continuities* with the anarchism of earlier epochs. In reality, neoanarchism re-encounters and reformulates some characteristics of anarchism that,

---

27 The zone à défendre (ZAD) is a militant eco-occupation movement, and later commune, first founded in the 2010s which successfully ended the threat of airport construction in the region.

while they practically disappeared after the defeat of the Revolution of 1936, did mark anarchism during the first third of the 20th century, above all in Spain. Thus for example, the desire to *transform the present* and to *transform oneself* without waiting for the revolution; or the effort to construct concrete alternatives to the system in multiple domains—such as education or production—or, also, the eagerness to tear away spaces from the system so as to be able to develop other ways of life;these were aspects that were constantly present from the end of the 19th century to the first third of the 20th century, in different countries, while they acquired a spectacular intensity in Spain after the Civil War began on July 19th 1936.

It is very likely that there exists a relationship between the current resurgence of anarchism and its *re-encounter* with principles that underpinned in its moments of greatest vigor. However, the terms "re-encounter" or "reinvent" should not be undervalued, because, in effect, it is not about *a mimesis*, a mere reproduction by imitation, but that these old principles are constructed in a new context which marks them with certain different characteristics. The existing continuities and similarities do not take away one iota of value from the process of *reinventing* and *reformulating by oneself,* instead of simply repeating, reproducing or receiving what is inherited.

THE REASONS FOR THE RESURGENCE/
RENEWAL OF ANARCHISM

Translators' note: Engaging directly with the contemporary resurgence and renewal of anarchism, Ibáñez aims in chapter three to conceptualise what he calls the "constitutively changeable" nature of the movement.

Binding together thought and action, anarchism develops within mutually sustaining relations between practice guided by and creative of ideas, and ideas generative of and resulting from practice. Historically, anarchism is particularly adept in relating its ideas directly to its practices, and this relationship between thought and action is paralleled at the broader level of the movement's relationship with any particular historical moment. Anarchism is made possible (as thought and practice) by the context from which it emerges, and changes that context in turn through its presence.

In other words, the anarchist movement's capacity to surge up anew depends on its renewal and its renewal depends on its capacity to produce the conditions of its own resurgence. And it is in this immanent to and fro between idea and practice, and between both and historical setting, that rebellious subjectivities are forged. Should these ties be severed, then anarchism and anarchists will only be found in libraries and museums.

If anarchism is surging again at the dawn of the 21st century, it is undoubtedly because the rapid social changes we have experienced in recent decades are in tune with some of its characteristics and a kind of concordance between specific aspects of reality and certain aspects of anarchism has thus been established. In other words, if some of the characteristics of contemporary sociopolitical, technological and cultural changes favour the deployment of certain anarchist practices, it is because there exists a certain similarity of process between these said characteristics and practices. As a result, it is in the interaction between these elements—that is, between, social changes and anarchism; but not in either considered separately. It is in the loop that anarchism forms with the changes that have been occurring where the secret of anarchism riding again is to be found.

Accordingly, for example, if we consider technological change it's clear that, parallel to the undeniable danger that they represent for our freedoms, NICTs (new information and communication technologies such as online social media, messaging services etc) also favour a horizontality of decision, exchange and relation, while increasing the possibilities of self-organisation and permitting rapid dissemination of local initiatives, to mention only a few of the effects these technologies have as they move in directions similar to that advocated or called for by anarchism.

Likewise, if we consider sociopolitical changes, it turns out that the expansion and growing sophistication of the procedures of control and exercises of power that are applied to ever more numerous aspects of our daily lives demonstrate that anarchism was completely correct in insisting on the existence of/importance of/significance of phenomena of power, and this contributes to increasing its credibility. Furthermore, this proliferation of microscopic interventions of power multiplies the occasions for deploying practices of resistance against domination, as anarchism maintains. Other changes, more circumstantial, such as the fall of the Berlin Wall in 1989 and the collapse of the Soviet Union, have also played a facilitating role in the development of anarchism. These events effectively put an end to Marxist hegemony in challenging capitalism and unblock the search for other references to direct contemporary radical politics.

Lastly, if we contemplate contemporary cultural changes we can see an ideology of modernity that is in crisis, particularly in its long-held "end of history" position that radical changes and forms of freedom beyond consumer capital are impossible. The failure of this globalised, totalising model can not help but reinforce anarchist positions.

Resurgence and renewal in one delivery

Before developing these themes, it is worthwhile to stop for a few moments to examine the fact that this is not only about a resurgence of anarchism, but also, simultaneously, about its renewal.

The resurgence and renewal of anarchism take place *in unison*. This is not surprising; the resurgence that we can presently verify is only possible because anarchism renews itself and is able, in this way, *to harness itself* to the new conditions which define the current epoch. Indeed, if it did not renew itself, no matter how favourable present conditions may be, it could not surge back again for the simple reason that these conditions are *unprecedented* in the path that anarchism has travelled so far. It is therefore necessary for anarchism to change to adapt itself to the new conditions and integrate the novelty that appears along its own journey. The very fact that it surges up again today indicates, in principle, that it has succeeded in carrying out enough of a renewal to be able to connect with changes that have occurred in its milieu. Therefore, *renewal is a necessary condition to render its resurgence possible*, but, at the same time, given that this resurgence articulates itself with the necessary adaptation to novel conditions, it cannot but reinforce, in turn, the renewal of what made it possible. Which means that *the resurgence of anarchism acts as a necessary condition that makes its own renewal possible.*

Resurgence and renewal form a continuous feedback loop linking back to the interaction between the characteristics of anarchism and those of specific social changes. To applaud the resurgence of anarchism and lament, at the same time, its movement away from its traditional forms — as some anarchists do and, even, some anarchist currents — constitutes therefore a contradiction that only becomes evident when the relationship between these two aspects is grasped. Here also a choice is imposed, because anarchism would not have been able to surge back again if it had remained unchanging. To oppose its renewal is to act, inevitably, against its reappearance.

While not forgetting that resurgence and renewal are mutually inseparable elements, I am now going to separate them for the purpose of exposition, presenting, firstly, a few considerations about the renewal of anarchism, following then with its resurgence.

The reasons for the renewal of anarchism

Anarchism as a constitutively changing reality

The renewal of anarchism is to be explained by its very *nature* as a changing reality, and not only *accidentally* so.

As time passes anarchism necessarily gathers to itself some of the new elements produced within it and is thereby more or less modified as a whole. That anarchism changes with the passage of time is evident, and in no way mysterious. It would be unusual if it stood still.

Anarchism however is not limited to experiencing *conjunctural* modifications, the outcome of historical avatars, but is a *constitutively* changing reality. This means that change is to be found *directly inscribed* in how it builds and maintains itself. Consequently, if change defines anarchism's *way of being*, it *could not continue to be what it is if it did not change.*

In other words, *anarchism is necessarily changeable* because its immutability would contradict *the kind of reality that it is.* This way of being is not without consequences because, for example, if what I put forth here is true, then there is nothing further removed from anarchism than to conceive it as a timeless, inalterable, immutable thing, defined once and for all. And this immediately pushes aside any pretension to watch over its original purity and any fancy to institute oneself as a guardian of the temple.

The reasons that render anarchism *constitutively* changeable rest principally on *the symbiosis between idea and action* that mark anarchist thought and practices.

As Proudhon and Bakunin clearly stated, *the idea* has as much an origin as a *practical* value; it is born in *a context of action* and is directed towards producing practical effects through the action that it in turn engenders. In this sense, anarchism, contrary to Marxism, is not an ensemble of analytical and programmatic texts that have the aim of guiding action, but a series of practices within which certain principles are manifest. These are principles that constitute themselves therefore through action, that are born from it and in turn steer it.

The symbiosis between *idea* and *action* is at the heart of the *constitutively* changeable character of anarchism. This is very easy to understand as soon as we look for a moment at what characterises action. Far from occurring in a vacuum or in the abstract, all action finds itself necessarily part of a historical context. As every historical context is, necessarily, specific and singular—precisely because it is historical—action that develops within it cannot but also be specific and singular and, therefore, change itself alongside the broader changes its historical context undergoes. A historical context which, behind each of the changes that it undergoes, is newly singular and specific, will demand consequently that the actions which develop within it be so as well, if they are to produce any kind of effect.

Of course, as action and idea are intimately bound in anarchism, the changes that action meets will produce, in turn, changes in the conceptual content of what action produces, and further action will be a consequence of those changes.

Ultimately, if anarchism was not able to change, breaking this tie between idea and action that comprises one of its formative elements, we would find ourselves looking at something that is anything but anarchism.

Anarchism did not preexist the practices that instituted it and it cannot survive beyond the practices that continuously produce it, except as a historical curiosity. It cannot do so because it is not something that inspires or activates these practices, that is latent below them, it is *these practices in themselves* and the principles that result from them.

The formation of anarchism in the struggles against domination

Anarchism can be defined, among other ways, as *that which contradicts the logic of domination, at whatever level it is deployed.* It is therefore in the midst of practices of struggle against domination that it forms. This indicates, yet again, that it necessarily evolves. In effect, these antagonistic practices cannot but transform themselves as a response to the course of history and the social changes that accompany it, the apparatuses and modalities of domination modifying and recomposing themselves.

If struggles are not born from nothing, but are provoked and defined by that *against which* they constitute themselves, then it can be inferred that it is *the new forms of domination* that have arisen in our society which inspire present day resistances and which bestow upon them their form. In other words, antagonistic movements neither invent themselves nor create that to which they are opposed; they only invent *the ways to oppose* these realities. So, for example, it is because the apparatuses of domination currently adopt reticular forms that the resistances also adopt them.

Stated differently, *that against which anarchism struggles changes* and, consequently, the forms of struggle also change giving way to new experiences and new approaches which, gathered to anarchism, make it evolve.

It also has to be taken into account that the new social conditions not only modify the apparatuses of domination and corresponding practices of struggle, but also produce modifications in the symbolic fabric and the cultural sphere. On the one hand, they give rise to new discourses of legitimation that are necessary to support these new apparatuses of domination, but, on the other, they also give rise to new analyses and new antagonistic discourses that enrich critical thought. That is, a modality of thought that, in the words of Foucault, puts into question all forms of domination, and that can be found, despite the enormous differences that separate them, across the works of Castoriadis, Deleuze[28], Foucault and Chomsky[29], among others.

Insofar as this way of thinking also constitutes a form of struggle against domination, it approaches and borders an anarchism that in turn must be influenced by it changing as it integrates some of the formulations of contemporary critical thought into its own discourse, as we will see in the chapter dedicated to postanarchism.

Ultimately, the only way to render anarchism invariant, fixed and stationary is to tear it away from the milieu in which it lives and embalm or mummify it, because living anarchism breaths in the fluidity of the change that animates it and, as said earlier, is ever "neither totally itself nor totally something other". It is a constitutively changeable way of being whose mode of existence consequently consists of finding itself in a perpetual becoming.

The reasons for the resurgence of anarchism

Among the changes that favour the growth of anarchism, I will only mention those related to the development of NICTs and, furthermore,

---

28 Gilles Deleuze (1925-1995) was a major French philosopher of the latter half of the 20th century. His work with Félix Guattari, including *Capitalism and Schizophrenia: Anti-Oedipus* and *A Thousand Plateaus* is particularly well known.

29 US linguistics professor Noam Chomsky is perhaps the best-known libertarian socialist academic of modern times. His decades-long work analysing State and media power has been widely praised and his book *Manufacturing Consent* is considered a modern classic.

those changes that result from the current proliferation of relations of power and the effects of domination.

NICTs, collective mobilisations and the self-institution of a new political subject

Although they contain evident freedom destroying features, it is obvious that the NICTs also enable a milieu favourable to the development of anarchist practices, facilitating horizontality, self-government and the exercise of direct democracy, while stimulating collective creativity and propitiating direct action.

A quick examination of popular mobilisations that have taken place these last years show that the use of NICTs impresses upon them characteristics that favour the expansion of anarchism. So, for example, the extraordinary rapidity and amplitude, sometimes surprising, of the mobilisations that are called through social networks (Facebook, Twitter, etc.) are possible because they aren't originating from or mediated by potent organisations, afflicted with all of the inertia and all of the weight that inevitably accompanies stable and lasting structures; and this confers on these mobilisations certain qualities that bring them close to libertarian modes of functioning. In effect, in the absence of a permanent centre of decision making and of pre-established structural frameworks, the initial call functions simply as a *trigger*, more than as an organising body, and leaves, thus, the essential part of the mobilisation and its success in the hands of the participants, depending on their sense of self-organisation and their initiative, which in these conditions, cannot but privilege horizontality and collective creativity.

Mobilisations that constitute themselves on social networks and via the NICTs have not displaced those that answer to the call of traditional organisations. Both today coexist, but, of course, they give rise to very different dynamics. Classical demonstrations can occasionally be seen to be overwhelmed and to take unpredictable directions, but in principle, everything falls under the control of the organisations that call them and the margin of initiative left in the hands of the participants is minimal. Preparations are long and labourious, prudence is obligatory because an eventual failure of participation represents certain costs for the organisation. By contrast, mobilisations called for without any stable organisational infrastructure can materialise in a way that is practically immediate, and what can happen escapes all control and all prediction. In general, these mobilisations often conclude without anything extraordinary happening, but sometimes the libertarian potentialities that characterise them gain form in very precise circumstances, as we shall see.

Certainly, the majority of popular mobilisations, both those of the past and those of today, have precise demands and maintain themselves as long as the collective energy that emanates from social discontent is sufficiently intense to sustain them. When this energy abates, either because results have been attained that diminish the discontent, or because of fatigue, dejection or repression, the mobilisation ceases and *a return to order* is produced, as the good people like to say.

Sometimes it happens that these struggles give way to the deployment of a collective creativity that puts into question and makes the very logic of the system falter. *A second kind of movement of rebellion* is thus outlined in which it can be seen that the thousands of people who invade the streets and public spaces do not do so only to protest against this or that particular aspect, or to demand this or that concrete measure, but also to institute or, better, to *self-create themselves as new political subjects*.

This process of self-institutionalisation that is carried out within such mobilisations demands that the people who organise themselves converse, collectively elaborate a political discourse that is proper to them, do whatever is necessary to keep the mobilisation going, and develop political action. This requires that the imagination be put to work to create spaces, construct conditions, and act in ways which enable people to set, by themselves and collectively, their own agenda at the margin of the watchwords that come from a place other than the mobilisation itself. This labour of creating a new political subject then takes the lead over the particular demands that provoked the initial mobilisation.

In this kind of situation, new social energies form alongside those of the original social discontent, feeding back upon themselves, losing intensity only, in the following instant, to grow back again, as in a storm. These energies rise up and constitute themselves within the very situations of confrontation. That is why great social uprisings have an unpredictable nature and come under the sign of spontaneity.

Subverting the status quo, occupying public spaces, transforming places of passage into zones of encounter and expression, all activate a collective creativity that invents, in each instant, new ways to extend subversion and have it proliferate.

Liberated spaces therefore illuminate new social relations which create, in turn, new social ties. People transform and politicise themselves in very little time, not superficially but profoundly, with incredible speed. It is, as a matter of fact, those concrete realisations, here and now, that reveal themselves as being capable of mobilising people, of inciting them to go further and to make them see that other ways of life are possible. However, for these realisations to see the light of day, it is necessary that people feel themselves to be protagonists, that they are deciding for themselves. And it is when they are truly protagonists and they really feel themselves to be so, that they involve themselves totally, exposing their bodies in the development of the struggle, thereby letting the movement of rebellion amplify itself well beyond what could have been predicted from the original discontent and confrontations. This process of self-institution *of a new political space, created in the very midst of struggles*, is very close to what anarchism advocates and calls for.

It was a phenomenon of this kind that occurred in Paris in May of 1968; long before, therefore, the existence of the *Internet* (which demonstrates that the NICTs are not necessary for these events to happen). It is also a phenomenon of this kind that filled the public squares of Spain with protesters from the 15th of May of 2011 on. All the same, what seems quite clear when we observe the struggles of the beginning of this century is that even though the NICTs are not, in any way, necessary for the formation of the conditions of collective creativity, direct democracy, and self-organisation, they do encourage their appearance, promoting mobilisations with a strongly libertarian character.

The proliferation of power and its reconceptualisation

In commenting on the reasons for its renovation and its formation in struggles, I said anarchism could be defined as *that which contradicts the logic of domination.* Anarchist thought has in effect put so much effort into unmasking the multiple damages that power inflicts on freedom and in delegitimising and dismantling the apparatuses of power, that it has instituted itself as *the ideology and the political thought of the critique of power,* while other emancipatory ideologies that originated in the 19th century confined this subject to a secondary or derivative level. It is precisely the importance given to the phenomenon of power that accounts for the vigorous actuality of anarchism. This modern incarnation harvests, so to speak, the fruits of the secular obstinacy with which anarchism has denounced the harmfulness of power and sees itself, finally, absolved of the accusation of having remained blind to the principal causes of injustice and exploitation, which some had situated exclusively in the economic sphere. However, we also have to recognise that in its questioning of power, anarchism has not always been correct.

In showing that relations of power are forged within social ties and that they are created incessantly throughout the very fabric of society, the research of Michel Foucault contradicted anarchist beliefs about the possibility of radically eliminating power, obliging a fairly profound reconsideration of this entire problem.

Paradoxically, the refutation of anarchism on this point seems to assure its permanence for a very long time, because if it is certain that relations of power are inherent to society and that *anarchism is fundamentally a desire to criticise, confront and subvert relations of power*, then something of what inspires anarchism cannot but persist while societies exist. And not because anarchism is called upon to actively perpetuate itself throughout the centuries, but because it is unlikely that a political current which, under different names or other modalities, continues to make the criticism of power its principal preoccupation whatever the concrete techniques adopted by domination, will completely disappear.

The political importance and active manifestation of anarchism has grown as the importance and sophistication of the relations of power in our daily lives has increased. In revealing the vast number of ways in which power is exercised today, and in questioning overly simplistic analyses that had previously rendered these invisible and thus shielded them from any possibility of contestation, Michel Foucault's research has contributed decisively to highlighting the extension of power and to magnifying its *perceived presence* in the social field. This has enormously *amplified* the field of anarchism's theoretical and practical intervention, underlying its importance.

However, it has not only been our perception of the modalities of the exercise of power that has been diversified and amplified in the last decades. We have also witnessed *an expansion of those aspects of our lives which are subject to the interventions of power.*

In contemporary society, power operates with an ever finer surgical precision, gaining access to the smallest details of our existence — so as to, among other things, extract surplus value — while at the same time increasing the areas in which it intervenes and the diversity of its procedures. Procedures that transform us, for example, into "entrepreneurs of the self", extending the logic of business to the whole social body, or which use our freedom to make us more competitive. With this multiplication of the facets of our existence that become targets of the interventions of power, the occasions for the concrete intervention of anarchism consequently multiply and, in parallel, the feeling that the exercise of power is an *omnipresent* phenomenon that should be a principal concern, as anarchism always affirmed, intensifies.

This omnipresence today awakens a more than justified anxiety that modern life continually feeds. The feeling that the apparatuses of power are in a position to control our most anodyne actions and that nothing can escape their gaze, finds ample sustenance in episodes such as WikiLeaks and Julian Assange[30], or Edward Snowden and the National Security Agency (NSA)[31] of the United States, as well as in the revelations about the use of *big data* to generate information and economic benefits from the traces we leave behind in the electronic fabric. Likewise, the procedures of continuous, exhaustive and "for always" recording and storage of online and mobile exchanges, accompanied by an unlimited capacity to treat this information, illustrate our already total transparency before the gaze of power. If to this we add the use of drones and other techniques for the physical elimination of individuals branded *undesirable*—poisonings, for example—power has gone well beyond, and without embarrassment, the control of information. The considerable expansion, in some parts of the population, of hostility to power and the desire to combat it, is understandable.

---

30 Whistleblower website Wikileaks, headed by Julian Assange, was hounded by the US government after it published, along with copious documentation on the Iraq war, a video dubbed *Collateral Murder* showing US troops laughing as they gunned people down from a helicopter. Assange was investigated on espionage charges in 2010, before being accused of sexual assault by two Swedish women in 2011 while living in Britain. Claiming political persecution, he sought asylum in Ecuador's London embassy, staying there from 2012-2019. At the time of print he is in prison in Britain, with a full US extradition hearing expected in 2020.

31 Edward Snowden leaked classified information showing widespread US government surveillance being used against its own citizens in 2013. He was subsequently accused of stealing government files and espionage, and fled to Russia where he has been granted political asylum and permanent settled status.

This extension of power also has a bearing on the world of work. Until a few decades ago, resistances were activated and armed on the bases of the conditions of exploitation that weighed upon the workers. Today these conditions continue to sustain important struggles. However, domination, which is much more diversified than in the past, has proliferated outside the field of productive labour, thereby considerably weakening the strength of the workers' movement. Today, it is not only a matter of extracting surplus value from labour power; all of the activities which workers give themselves over to, outside their workplaces, also produce benefits for capital to a degree and with a diversity of procedures previously unknown. Their savings, capitalistic leisure, their health, their houses, the education of their children, care given and received, etc., produce dividends that, while always substantial, have grown exponentially in recent times.

It is thus not surprising that the coming to political awareness increasingly originates from experiences of *control exercised over our daily lives* and in the perception that *our whole existence is commodified*. It is from this experience and this perception that the new antagonistic and radical subjectivities of our time grow.

It is helpful therefore to consider both the critical thought that is contributing to a new analysis of the relations of power, and the characteristics of how power is exercised in contemporary society, to see that the field that opens up before anarchist struggle is experiencing a spectacular deployment.

The social, cultural, political and technological changes of these last decades are creating conditions favourable to a resurgence of anarchism, while at the same time obliging it to renew a certain number of its presuppositions and perspectives. On the level of practices, this renewal has taken on, in good measure, the form of what I earlier called *neoanarchism*, while on a more theoretical level, it has taken on, in part, the form of *postanarchism*, as we will see in what follows.

POSTANARCHISM

Translators' note: The penultimate chapter of Anarchism is Movement directly engages with debate over the significance of "postanarchism". Neither tempted by blind adherence, nor categorically dismissive, Ibáñez attempts to navigate between these extremes, always attentive to the complex relations between theory and practice that animate anarchism.

Strongly criticised by some, praised by others, postanarchism currently enjoys a presence in the international anarchist movement significant enough that it can no longer be ignored.

The term *postanarchism* probably first appeared in March of 1987 when Hakim Bey—pseudonym for Peter Lamborn Wilson—published a very short text with the title *Post-Anarchism Anarchy*. It would however be a big mistake if we thought to locate in this manifesto the point of departure for postanarchism as it has subsequently developed. Bey's text is a plea against the paralysing effects caused by the fossilisation of anarchist organisations and against the sclerosis of anarchism converted into, according to him, a mere ideology. It is a call to *overtake anarchism in the name of anarchy*, but the conceptual lines of what would subsequently constitute postanarchism do not appear. In fact, Bey's influence will be noticed, above all, among certain sectors of neoanarchism more than in postanarchism, with notions of the "*TAZ*" and "*PAZ*"—"Temporary Autonomous Zones" and "Permanently Autonomous Zones", respectively—which he highlighted in the 1990s influencing segments of libertarian occupations and insurrectionism.

Where does postanarchism come from what does it consist of?

Paradoxically, it is in a work that did not mention the term postanarchism anywhere that its origin can be located. Todd May, a US anarchist and academic, published in 1994 a book titled *The Political Philosophy of Poststructuralist Anarchism* which clearly announced what would constitute one of the essential dimensions of postanarchism, namely, the inclusion within it of important conceptual elements taken from poststructuralism. May had already touched on the concept in 1989 with an article entitled 'Is Post-Structuralist Political Theory Anarchist?'. Published in a philosophy journal of limited circulation however, it went largely unnoticed. The same happened with an article entitled 'Poststructuralism and the Epistemological Bases of Anarchism", published in 1993 by another university professor, Andrew Koch, again in a philosophy journal with modest circulation.

A few years later, while the echoes of the great demonstration of 1999 in Seattle still resonated with force, offering testimony to the resurgence of anarchism, another book, in which the term *postanarchism* is also not used, took up in part May's theoretical argument. This book, published in 2001 by Australian anarchist professor Saul Newman, titled *From Bakunin to Lacan: Anti-Authoritarianism and the Dislocation of Power*, ends with a chapter textually calling for "a postanarchist politics", employing the instruments of poststructuralism.

In the following year, 2002, another Californian professor, Lewis Call, published a work along the same lines, *Postmodern Anarchism*, which reinforced a current for which three possible denominations now competed: first, "poststructuralist anarchism", second, "postmodern anarchism" and as a third option, "postanarchism". It was this last denomination, despite being the least precise, the most ambiguous and the most problematic, that finally imposed itself. The first phrase would have been undoubtedly the most appropriate and the most precise, carrying with it a direct reference to poststructuralism, but it was too tied to university culture. The final result was also probably influenced by the discredit that had undermined the term "postmodern", due to its vague content, changing definitions, and the sometimes contradictory character of its political implications.

It is possible that the creation, in February 2003 by Jason Adams—an organiser of the Seattle demonstrations—of a website called *Post Anarchism*, which served as a platform for numerous exchanges and debates, contributed to spreading and consolidating the use of this term. In any case, the publications and the references to postanarchism have continued to multiply since then and in 2011, a mere ten years after the publication of Saul Newman's book, there was already the first *Post-Anarchism Reader*.

When the texts that develop or discuss postanarchist approaches are reviewed, what appears with the greatest force is perhaps the idea of a *hybridisation* of anarchism and poststructuralism, or the inclusion of poststructuralist concepts within anarchism. It is the grafting, some would say, of poststructuralism onto anarchism that will make way for a new variety of libertarian formulations, giving form to postanarchism.

Jason Adams states, for example, that postanarchism is not so much a coherent political program, but rather an anti-authoritarian problematic which stems from an anarchist poststructuralist approach or, even, from a poststructuralist anarchist approach.

Benjamin Franks writes that postanarchism is to be understood as a new hybrid of anarchism and poststructuralism. Saul Newman presents it as the construction of an intersection between anarchism and poststructuralist discourse. Franks adds that the term postanarchism, used more often than not with a certain hesitation, refers to an ensemble of efforts to reinvent anarchism in light of the principal developments that have marked contemporary radical theory and that began, in many cases, with the events of May '68 in Paris.

On the opening page of Adams' site, below the heading 'What is postanarchism?', he states:

> *In order to understand what the emerging phenomena of postanarchism "is" in the contemporary moment, first of all one should consider what it is not; it is not an "ism" like any other — it is not another set of ideologies, doctrines and beliefs that can be laid out positively as a bounded totality to which one might conform and then agitate amongst the "masses" to get others to rally around and conform to as well, like some odd ideological flag.*
>
> *Instead, this profoundly negationary term refers to a broad and heterogeneous array of anarchist theories and practices that have been rendered "homeless" by the rhetoric and practice of most of the more closed and ideological anarchisms such as anarchist-syndicalism, anarchist-communism, and anarchist-platformism as well as their contemporary descendants, all of which tend to reproduce some form of class-reductionism, state-reductionism or liberal democracy in a slightly more "anarchistic" form, thus ignoring the many lessons brought to us in the wake of the recent past.*
>
> *Postanarchism is today found not only in abstract radical theory but also in the living practice of such groups as the No Border movements, People's Global Action, the Zapatistas, the Autonomen and other such groups that while clearly "antiauthoritarian" in orientation, do not explicitly identify with anarchism as an ideological tradition so much as they identify with its general spirit in their own unique and varying contexts, which are typically informed by a wide array of both contemporary and classical radical thinkers.*

...

[In] Saul Newman['s] ... book From Bakunin to Lacan:
Antiauthoritarianism and the Dislocation of Power ... *the term
refers to a theoretical move beyond classical anarchism, into a hybrid
theory consisting of a synthesis with particular concepts and ideas from
poststructuralist theory, such as post-humanism and anti-essentialism.*
(Jason Adams, *Postanarchism in a Nutshell*)

We conclude this brief review taking up what Newman, undoubtedly the
principal theorist of postanarchism, argues:

*This does not, in any sense, refer to a superseding or moving beyond
of anarchism—it does not mean that the anarchist theoretical and
political project should be left behind ... The prefix "post-" does not
mean "after" or "beyond", but rather a working at the conceptual limits
of anarchism with the aim of revising, renewing and even radicalising
its implications.*
– Saul Newman, *Post-Anarchism and Radical Politics Today*[32]

Given the poststructuralist and postmodern affiliations of postanarchism,
one could expect that this latter would likewise take up the offensive
against the legitimising ideology of modernity, but directing criticism
against modern presuppositions that would eventually dwell in anarchist
thought. And, indeed, postanarchists endeavour to show that anarchism is
very far from having escaped from the ideological influences of modernity.

---

32 *Translators' Note*: The website that Ibáñez mentions, created by Jason Adams in 2003, no
longer seems to exist. Instead of therefore translating Ibáñez's own translation of Adams'
text, I have quoted from a piece by Adams entitled *Postanarchism in a Nutshell* (available
online at the Anarchist Library), which seems to repeat the passage quoted by Ibáñez.
The passage quoted by Saul Newman appears in the book without any direct reference.
I have then assumed that it is quoted from Newman's essay *Post Anarchist and Radical
Politics Today*.

It seems to me that we cannot but agree with them on this point — on the condition, of course, that we refuse to conceive of anarchism as something which sprung up from a preexisting foundational essence and think of it instead as having constituted itself through an ensemble of historically rooted social and cultural practices. These practices were not in fact those of a few isolated individuals, but were developed by thousands of people who were fundamentally — and how the devil could it be otherwise? — *modern subjects*, given that it is in the Modern Epoch that anarchism constituted itself as a significant social movement.

Logically, anarchism cannot but be profoundly marked by the social conditions and fundamental ideas of modernity. Of course, anarchism is not a faithful copy of the principles of modernity, as some postanarchists sometimes insinuate. And it is not for various reasons, such as, the fact that modernity's dominant character is not homogenous and incorporates many influences, in this precise case, Enlightenment ideologies and those that emanate from Romanticism.

Anarchism in fact sees itself influenced by modernity twice over. First, because it develops historically within modernity and absorbs some of its characteristics. Secondly, because it incorporated certain practices of struggle against certain aspects of modernity. Anarchism situates itself consequently, *in modernity and against modernity*, to take up the expression of Nico Berti[33] when he speaks of anarchism as something that is *in history but against history*.

Consequently, anarchism constructs itself by at the same time opposing certain aspects of modernity and equally, accommodating it. With some frequency, it happens that *with and against* are not incompatible and this is what occurs here, given that, on the one hand, anarchist practices articulate themselves against particular mechanisms of domination

---

33 Italian scholar GIampetro "Nico" Berti is the author of numerous texts on anarchism who in his work on "the new masters" in the 1970s identified the rise of a political techno-bureaucracy, or what we know today as technocrats.

of modernity, but on the other, they construct themselves necessarily with materials and with tools specific to their time. They are therefore *simultaneously modern and anti-modern practices.*

The idea that anarchism finds itself inevitably marked by the spirit and the social conditions of its time in fact follows logically from a conception of anarchism that understands its theoretical corpus on the basis of certain practices of struggle and, above all, practices of struggle against domination. The idea that anarchism could move through modernity without being influenced by it could only be sustained by an essentialist conception of anarchism, or on the basis of a mysterious capacity that anarchism would have to have in order to transcend the conditions that constitute it.

Allowing then that the postanarchist thesis, according to which anarchism has incorporated certain influences originating in modernity, is reasonable, we can now ask ourselves about the conditions that have allowed postanarchists to conclude this and to constitute themselves as a distinct current of thought within anarchism. It is of course in the social, economic, cultural and political changes of the second half of the 20th century that these conditions of possibility are to be found; that is, finally, in the same phenomena that caused the resurgence of anarchism.

These changes effectively mark the beginning of a transition in our societies towards forms and conditions of existence which we are experiencing for the first time, but which increasingly differentiate themselves from those that characterised most of "modernity"; a period that begins to gain shape during the 16th century, creates its legitimising ideology during the century of the Enlightenment, and which continues to be for the most part ours today, even though it has ceased to be hegemonic. (For a more elaborate development of the question of modernity and postmodernity, see *Addendum 1*.)

In parallel to the technological, political and economic changes that have fuelled a recomposition of the apparatuses and modalities of domination and, therefore, of struggles, the second half of the 20th century has seen a movement develop that is strongly critical of modernity's legitimising ideology. This critique has antecedents in the Enlightenment — in Romanticism, for example — and, later, in its opponents such as Max Stirner or Friedrich Nietzsche[34]; a critical movement that from the 1980s on, came to be called postmodern thought or poststructuralist theory.

The conditions for the possibility of postanarchism thus lie in the development of poststructuralist/postmodern criticism, which for its part is made possible by *the first steps towards a change of epoch.*

The inclusion of postanarchism in the critical movement that rails against certain aspects of modern ideology offers some credence to the idea that this approach does not originate with concrete struggles and is ultimately no more than an intellectual movement, strictly academic. If we look more closely, however, it is apparent that its formulation and development relate, though indirectly, with current struggles against domination. On the one hand, May '68 and, more generally, the struggles that erupted in the world at the end of the 1960s and the beginning of the 1970s are not foreign to the elaboration of poststructuralist and postmodernist analysis, upon which postanarchism rests. On the other hand, postanarchism would not have found any echo and, perhaps, would not even have been formulated, without the eruption of practices and forms of intervention that are specific to radical politics as they have configured themselves from the end of the 1990s until the present.

It is true that postanarchism invents absolutely nothing, that it takes its tools from the theoretical spaces of poststructuralism and postmodernism. It is enough to see the importance that it gives to the anarchist criticism of representation, or the anarchist exaltation of diversity and singularity,

---

34 Max Stirner (1806-1856) is perhaps the best-known exponent of individualist theory, particularly via *The Ego and its Own*, while Friedrich Nietsche (1844-1900) was one of the most important philosophical figures of his era, particularly in his considerations of atheism, nihilism and the will to power.

to be convinced of the origin of its tools. Nevertheless, it is also true that postanarchism contributes to making this criticism known in anarchist milieus and this is a great merit, even if it is finally its only merit.

It would however be erroneous to reduce postanarchism to the simple role of disseminator of concepts and theses, because postanarchism also presents itself as an effort at self-criticism that realises anarchism by freeing it from its past debts to the legitimising ideology of modernity. Of course, if the usefulness of the Enlightenment in undermining the conceptions, institutions and practices of subjugation that existed at that time leaves no room for doubt, nor can it be ignored that the social changes that have occurred over the course of modernity and the labour carried out by critical thought have made ever more visible the subtle effects of subjugation that the ideas of the Enlightenment also bore. And these can no longer be simply assumed, without further ado, by antagonistic movements.

The criticism of classical anarchism

Among the many criticisms that postanarchism directs at anarchism, two of the most important are over its essentialist suppositions and its overly old-fashioned conception of power. The latter fails to take into consideration, among other things, the *productive* nature and the *immanence* that characterise modern expressions of power. Even though I have moved a more detailed exposition on the problematics of power and essentialism to the *Addendum 2*, I would like to briefly address the theme of essentialism, considering it exclusively in its relation to *the question of the subject*, which will inevitably touch on some aspects of the problematic of power.

It is in fact obvious that anarchism shares, in good measure, the modern belief in the existence of *an autonomous subject*, and that it would be sufficient to pluck it from the claws of power for it to be able to finally realise itself, to be free and *to act for itself*. It is thus about working for *the emancipation* of individuals. That is, to act to remove them from tutelage, from servitude or, at least, the ensemble of restrictions that repress them, so as to finally own oneself. However, poststructuralism teaches us that *beneath the paving stones there is no beach*, that there is not a desire we can liberate or a subject to be emancipated, because once there was we would not see an *autonomous* being, but a being *already moulded and constituted by relations of power*. To oppose the effect of the apparatuses of domination will never reveal a constitutively autonomous subject that, liberated from what repressed it, would find *its authentic self*, for the reason that this *self* does not exist. All we can hope for, and it is not a small thing, is that the subject independently finds the instruments to modify and reconstitute itself differently, neither closer nor further from what would be its fundamental nature, for this last is to be found nowhere—*it simply does not exist*.

Saul Newman argues that one of the most perverse effects of Enlightenment ideology, and its humanist presuppositions, was the construction of subjectivities that perceived themselves as endowed with an "essence" which would be repressed by the actions of certain external circumstances. This perception effectively guides the struggle against power in a direction that paradoxically *reinforces it*, given that the struggle to liberate our essence from what represses it seeks to liberate something which in fact is already constituted by power. Instead of scrutinising the marks left behind by its interventions, we assume them as alien to power and as something which preexists its action. This ultimately opens the door to the normalising effects that produce a belief in *human nature* which would be—with apologies for redundancy—purely "natural". Certainly, if a human nature exists and if we wish to be recognised and recognise ourselves as "human subjects", we should try to mould ourselves as faithfully as possible to its defining characteristics and norms, without anyone even asking this of us, simply allowing certain normalising effects to act.

With the crisis of the autonomy of the subject, ideologies of emancipation are thus also seen as invalid, in many respects. In addition to what presented itself as the autonomous subject needing to be emancipated, the subject charged with carrying out that emancipation (the proletariat) also became problematic, while doubts began to grow regarding the ultimate objectives of emancipatory struggle; that is, the creation of a pacified and reconciled society, in the purest utopian tradition.

These critical developments have led us to the necessity of redefining radical politics. Not to disarm them, as is feared by the defenders of ideologies anchored in the 19th century, but to *rearm them* with the aim of increasing their effectiveness in a modern society. For example, there is no doubt of the continued necessity of fighting against the State, as long as this continues to be the principal apparatus of repression and control. It is however necessary to abandon, among other things, the naive belief that the State only exercises power from above, on subjects whose only tie to it would be rooted in the fact that they are trapped by its nets and suffer its dominion. In reality, these bonds are far more dense than can be inferred from a mere subordination, given that the State acquires some of its features from below, in this case, as a consequence of the effects of power produced by subjects themselves in the context of their relations. In being partly shaped by its subjects, it is natural that the State shares some of their attributes without demanding any coercion. Therefore, to struggle against the State also consists of changing things "below" in local, diverse and situated practices, where power acquires some of its attributes.

It would be extremely interesting for anarchism to appropriate and integrate the poststructuralist-postmodern critique into its own critical baggage, above all in its Foucauldian variant. Among other things, this variant teaches us about what constitutes us today and what, because of the very fact that it constitutes us, escapes our view. This can help us to understand what underpins our thought, practices, subjectivities and libertarian sensibilities. Such understanding may help to better focus our struggles against domination.

To limit oneself to protecting the modern elements of anarchism is as useless as the effort to place value on the differences that separate it from modernity. What is truly important is to give to anarchism expressions that are at one with the present. That is, with an epoch that is still massively modern, certainly, but where the advances of postmodernity are more visible with each passing day.

Nevertheless, it is in no way the debate over postanarchism that will be decisive for reaching this goal, but the changes experienced through struggles against domination. In effect, to the extent that anarchism, as I do not stop repeating, constructs itself on the bases and in the midst of these practices of struggle, it follows that it necessarily changes with them. It is, consequently, because *it indissolubly joins idea and action*, because it establishes *a symbiosis between theory and practice*, that anarchism engenders new ideas when it engages with new practices, thereby renewing itself on both planes at once.

Whether we are conscious of it or not, anarchism is surreptitiously becoming postmodern, in the first place because it remains determined to combat all forms of domination; in the second, because domination modifies its own features with the advance of postmodernity, and in the third, because anarchism does not separate its theoretical formulations from its practices of struggle. And it does so as a consequence of its adaptation to the characteristics of the present. It is needless to say that this is eminently positive, as much to assure the political future of anarchism, as to maintain in all of their intensity the struggles against domination.

The criticism of postanarchism

These quite favourable considerations with regards to postanarchism should not make us lose sight of the fact that it has been the object of strong criticisms from the anarchist movement, and that some of these criticisms are not without foundation. There are, roughly, two types of critical considerations.

The first, formulated by numerous anarchists, among them Jesse Cohn and Wilburg Shawn[35], believe that classical anarchism and postanarchism in fact differ little and maintain that to justify the existence of postanarchism, its defenders insist on deforming and making a caricature of classical anarchism, of which they certainly have an insufficient overall knowledge. Thus, postanarchists would trace a biased image of anarchism with the aim of demonstrating the importance of reforming it in the light of poststructuralism, and for this they resort to selecting fragments of chosen authors who are far from representative of the breadth and diversity of anarchist thought that assumes perhaps some presuppositions originating with Enlightenment ideology, but is not uncritical of it.

In her book on contemporary anarchism, Vivien García[36] reproaches postanarchists not only for important gaps in their knowledge of anarchism, but also for misinterpreting its nature, succumbing to the professional deformation produced by their academic activity. This being a problem that impedes them from seeing that the texts of anarchism, indivisible from their involvement in political action, cannot be dealt with as if they formed a theoretical corpus of a principally philosophical kind.

Others seek to deactivate the charge against modern predispositions of anarchism claiming, as Nathan Jun[37] does, that classical anarchism was already postmodern and had anticipated notions emphasised only much later by poststructuralists. Jun's thesis is that the ideas of Proudhon, Bakunin and other anarchist thinkers, among which he highlights of course Max Stirner, are in the end quite close to those of Friedrich

---

35 Jesse Cohn and Wilburg Shaw co-authored *What's Wrong With Postanarchism?* In 2002.
36 Published in 2007, *L'Anarchisme Aujourd'hui* (Anarchism Today) sees Garcia analyse and critique postanarchism.
37 Nathan Jun is a US academic specialising in 19th and 20th century anarchist theory. Among many other works he co-edited *New Perspectives on Anarchism* in 2009.

Nietzsche, and that it is the ideas of Nietzsche that influence Foucault or Deleuze.

The second type of criticism, originating above all with platformists[38] (to structure, in a more cohesive way, organised anarchism) and also with certain libertarian communist currents, believes that postanarchism is an approach that unconsciously plays the game of neoliberalism and thus turns anarchism away from struggles rooted in the world of labour. This criticism, formulated principally by Michael Schmidt and Lucien van der Walt in their book *Black Flame*[39] is already found in embryo in the works of Murray Bookchin and in John Zerzan[40]. As Newman notes, Bookchin and Zerzan attack poststructuralism on various grounds and with different objectives, but their central thesis is that poststructuralism — because it puts into question the autonomy of the subject and the liberatory potential of Enlightenment rationality — implies a kind of nihilist irrationalism which, according to them, renders it impossible to be ethically and politically committed and leads it finally to have conservative implications.

If one in fact follows the writings of Saul Newman over the course of these last years, one can see that the first type of criticism, formulated shortly after postanarchism emerged, has had a certain effect on the theses developed by him. It has softened, so to speak, his criticism of classical anarchism, attenuating his recriminations against its modern

---

38 Supporters, to varying degrees, of a concept first attempted through the *Organisational Platform of the Libertarian Communists*, a document produced primarily by Nestor Makhno, Ida Mett and Peter Arshinov in 1926 which attempted to practically cohere anarchist ideals into a single organisational model. The concept was hotly debated at the time and remains controversial.

39 *Black Flame* (2009) attempted an overview of 150 years of anarchism through the lens of class struggle. The title was well recieved on publication but overshadowed in 2015 after co-author Michael Schmidt was exposed as having advocated the merging of anarchist and white supremacist ideas both privately under his own name and publicly under pseudonyms.

40 John Zerzan is one of the best-known exponents of anarcho-primitivism, which takes the view that technology itself is humanity's greatest failings. His major work is *Against Civilization: Readings and Reflections*.

elements, and has had him pay greater attention to the continuities rather than the oppositions between both types of anarchism. It is somewhat as if postanarchism recognised that it had a tendency to overestimate the impact of Enlightenment ideology on anarchism and to exaggerate the reach of its critical absorption of the essentialism that accompanies it.

We see then that postanarchism has not turned a deaf ear to criticisms, showing its openness to reacting positively to some of them. Furthermore, it has demonstrated its vitality by continuing to feed a critical debate within anarchism, and by endeavouring to reach out to the various contemporary expressions of practices of struggle as well as to the theoretical elaborations of radical politics, as developed within, but also outside, the anarchist tradition. In this sense, queer theory, postmarxism, the work of Judith Butler[41], Jacques Rancière[42], Toni Negri[43] or the Tiqqun current, to cite only a few examples, are taken into account, so as to approach them critically and, also, to collect elements capable of enriching postanarchism and converting it into a space of anarchist intellectual creativity.

---

41 Butler's philosophical work has been hugely influential especially on third wave feminist theory. Her best-known book *Gender Trouble: Feminism and the Subversion of Identity* analyses gender as a performative phenomenon.
42 Rancière is a French philosopher who has worked extensively on the question of how philosophers interact with the poor and concepts of the working class.
43 Negri is the co-author of *Empire* with Michael Hardt.

LIBERTARIAN PROSPECTIVE

In the preceding pages, I have tried to describe some of the forms in which contemporary anarchism presents itself and have suggested a few hypotheses with the aim of endeavouring to understand what has given it a new vitality at the beginning of this century. These hypotheses are of course completely debatable and the conception of anarchism upon which they rest may provoke agreement or arguments. However, in light of the successive episodes of rebellion in the world, it seems to me quite clear that anarchism in these last years surges anew with force, that it does so in a significantly renewed form and that *this resurgence and this renewal are intimately bound up with each other*. In other words, one does not go without the other, and this is for reasons that are neither due to mere circumstances nor to accidents, but refer instead, as I have tried to show, to essential issues.

With everything, it must still be asked if the form that contemporary anarchism is acquiring, made up of a mixture of neoanarchism, of anarchism beyond its own limits, and postanarchism, constitutes in the end a subculture that will add itself to those which already exist — individualism, libertarian communism, anarcho-syndicalism, insurrectionism etc. Or if, on the contrary, we can consider it as the prefiguration of a new modality of radical politics that will take up anew the fundamental intuitions of anarchism, recomposing them in an original way. My conviction is that this new radical politics will gain shape, slowly, and will come to substitute, in a more or less long term, that which began in the 19th century. However, I have no certain criterion as to whether this new political radicality is prefigured in contemporary anarchism.

Like the famous Russian dolls that fit one into the other, various elements today come together to explain the double movement of anarchism's resurgence and renewal, and at the same time to offer some clues as to the grounds on the basis of which it can continue to develop and achieve a real influence on our societies or, at least, on some significant parts of them.

A first aspect is in the extraordinary importance of *the imaginary* in the mobilisation of affects, to create a feeling of community, to stoke the desire to struggle and to activate, eventually, movements of rebellion. In effect, one has to intensely believe that another, better order of things is possible and fervently desire its manifestation, in order to commit oneself without reservation to the struggle to change existing reality.

The recognition of the importance of the imaginary is nothing new; its role however seems to increase significantly in present day subversive movements. Being starved of certain material and/or symbolic goods sometimes becomes so unbearable that people lose all fear and openly commit themselves to the struggle to change things. It may also be, nevertheless, that the collective imaginary is the principal cause and motor of rebellions. Struggle and commitment however are not self-sufficient values; to fight in the name of convictions and an ideal are not necessarily laudable, as the struggles driven by fascist or jihadist imaginaries remind us. Obviously, everything depends on, ultimately, why one struggles and what we are committed to. The kind of imaginary capable of promoting struggles with a libertarian character takes the form of *utopia*. Utopia can be understood as a principle which activates and revitalises the radical rejection of the world imposed upon us, even as, with greater or lesser precision, the outlines of what we desire, or at least the values upon which what is desired should be based, are traced.

The current resurgence of anarchism is accompanied by a revalorisation of utopian thought and by the conviction of the necessity of utopia. Perhaps because in part the present world lacks any utopia, anarchism finds a propitious breeding ground for its development. These circumstances point to the sustenance and intensification of the *urgency of utopia* as a possible ground for the development of anarchism. However, just as it is said, jokingly, that nostalgia is not what it used to be, it turns out that utopia is also not exactly what it was in the past. If we observe with care the renewal of anarchism, we can see that the current revitalisation of utopia is the revitalisation of *a utopia fully conscious of being so*, absolutely convinced that it is *nothing more* than a utopia; that is, aware that it is only *an incitement* to struggle and not *a future project in search of realisation*. This is a demand for utopia as the receptacle of our desires and of our dreams, as the place for the expression of a more encouraging vision of the world and as a navigation map, blurred and imprecise, where the routes have *to be invented* rather than *followed*.

It is consequently a kind of utopia liberated from all of the end-times visions that accompanied it far too frequently in the old revolutionary imaginary, a utopia that has bid a final farewell to the siren songs that promised a better future, if the present were sacrificed, and which only point to the future as a mere orientation to *actively construct present reality*. Because it is in our daily life that people have *to live the revolution*. In fact, either we experience it and live it from now on, or, what is more probable, we will never come to know it. A phrase comes to me in this instant, without knowing its source. It more or less said: "life is what passes while we prepare ourselves to live, it is what flows while we plan life projects". In like manner, the revolution will pass out to sea and it will remain beyond our reach if we do not anchor it firmly in the present.

It may seem incongruent, or even contradictory, to connect so directly something which opens onto the future, as *utopia* does, with a prosaic preoccupation about *the present*, and readers might suspect that I have let myself be carried away with oxymorons. Nonetheless, the extraordinary *dilation of the present,* which is for new generations the only truly significant part of a time where the past and present are confined to ever narrower margins, undoubtedly represents one of the most significant phenomena of an epoch when the piercing cry "No Future" resonates. Whether we celebrate the preeminence conceded to the present because it raises itself up against the ingenuous and submissive acceptance of its sacrifice on the altar of the future, or we regret this so called preeminence because it makes long-term political projects so difficult, it is clear that emergent anarchism and, more generally, radical politics, *express themselves today in the present.* In effect, today's oppositional movements demand that political proposals be judged in terms of their immediate suitability for really existing situations. It is for this reason that, to my understanding, the preeminence attributed to the present constitutes a second possible ground for the development of anarchism.

In this case however it is also necessary to avoid a possible misunderstanding. The presentism which characterises a good part of contemporary anarchism must not be interpreted as if the objective of struggle is to create spaces where one can live relatively well and in line with anarchist values, while the rest of humanity lives in unbearable conditions. This would imply that there is little which differentiates the values of anarchism from the principles which animate capitalism. In the same way that no one is really free while there are those who are not, neither can one live in harmony with libertarian principles while others remain exploited and oppressed. Emphasis is not placed on the present so as to attain a certain, more satisfactory, *way of being*[44] — but to articulate a mode of struggle. This emphasis simply means that the trap of postponing the actual transformation of reality with the aim of dedicating all of one's

---

44 Even though the fact of living according to our principles, of being consistent with ourselves and of seeking to resolve the contradictions that the surrounding world imposes on us, also makes us feel better.

energies to pure confrontation is rejected. This trap hides the fact that the transformation of the present is, before anything else, a weapon and, perhaps, one of the most dangerous for the system because it eats away at it from within and permits its relentless harassment.

Likewise, an emphasis on the present which ignores the past would, through naivety, make itself extremely vulnerable, if it broke all ties with the memory of earlier struggles and with the accumulated experiences of the long confrontation with domination. To centre on the present does not mean constantly starting from zero and having to newly learn and experiment with everything. The historical legacy of social movements against oppression and exploitation is too rich not to seek and learn from it in order to effectively shake up the present. It is precisely because they know that collective memory is the bearer of tremendously dangerous weapons for its survival that the dominant powers of society take such great efforts to bury and distort it.

The modern mix of utopia and radical presentism, paradoxically united in contemporary anarchism, are accompanied by a third element that grows daily as an instrument of resistance and subversion against the status quo, while also increasing the draw of anarchism. This has to do with its *constructive capacity*, something which completes the diverse practices of confrontation that it encourages and the will to resist that it inspires.

Anarchism must not only offer reasons and means for struggle, it also has to offer *reasons to live in a different way* and the means to experience, in practice, a different life. It is precisely because it is able to offer all of this *today* that it is able to seduce minority and increasingly larger youth elements. Its constructive capacity makes it possible to tear away spaces from the system, and to construct modes of life capable of offering more satisfactions than those offered by the mirages of commodity consumerism and to oppose the latter's power of seduction. It is in this constructive capacity where anarchism finds, I believe, a third ground for its development.

A fourth condition consists of the necessity to definitively abandon all *totalising* pretensions, rediscovering the suspicion already long manifested by classical anarchist individualism, even though this based its caution on the demand that all singularities be respected and not on the present arguments.

Against totalising temptations, anarchists must in fact be fully convinced that their values, their ideas, their practices, their utopias, their beliefs, the ways of life they long for, in sum, all that distinguishes and characterises them will never be able, far from it, to reach *unanimity* in an extraordinarily diverse humanity.

They must accept, without any reticence or the least bitterness, that choices different from their own are perfectly legitimate and that the only rationally conceivable social reality is *a plural and heterogeneous reality*, in which it will represent only a more or less limited part of humanity and in which it will find itself in a context of *necessary coexistence* with other options.

It is a matter then of acting and working "with others", in struggles and in everyday life, and to open oneself up to ideas and experiences coming from *outside* our own tradition. To do things with others who do not exactly share all of our modes of being and thinking, not because of the mere tactical preoccupation of increasing our forces to better struggle against the enemy, but, as I said before, for reasons of principle, because anarchism is also *the respect of and search for diversity in freedom*. And it should be concretely, in a situation and in practice, that the limits of this common activity and this shared everyday life should be evaluated, because if, effectively, it is certain that other options are perfectly legitimate, it is no less certain that ours are also equally so, and that *we have the full right to defend them*. To defend them without imposing them, of course, "to be an anarchist obliges" — as our comrade André Bernard says — yet without accepting, as well, impositions from others, and without hesitating to resort to force, if necessary, to impede such (see the *addenda* dedicated to relativism).

As it is not advisable to live in a ghetto we will have no other remedy but to find ways to reconcile living in as libertarian a milieu *as is possible* with, on the other hand, the necessity of *coexisting with other milieus.* This is one of the challenges that anarchism has to resolve and that is posed not only at the global level of a society, but, even, in the micro-spaces that we are able today to wrench away from the system. Along these same lines, it should be stressed that anarchism should be more sensitive to its own cultural and civilisational determinants, be fully conscious of its undeniable Eurocentrism and Christian-influenced roots. It is indispensable that anarchism establish a dialogue, an exchange and a confrontation with related but culturally-distinct perspectives, so as to be able to critically rethink some of the presuppositions that shape it and to make them less dependent on its socio-cultural determinants.

The problematic of power and domination, which has become much more sensitive than in the past and which provokes evermore numerous and vehement reactions of resistance from some youth, constitutes a fifth element that explains the recovery of vitality of the ideology which historically concerned itself, in the most determined way, with this issue.

In parallel, the increasing weight of power on the social fabric has considerably enriched analysis of this phenomenon, giving way to a new understanding of its mechanisms. This is certainly a new understanding that obliges anarchism to qualify and, sometimes, to reconsider in depth its own conceptions of power. This has contributed to its renewal, even though the influence of its old conceptions continues to be excessive.

Finally, a sixth element that appears in anarchism's resurgence and renewal — if only explicitly addressed by the postanarchist current — is the mistrust shown towards a good number of the presuppositions of the legitimising ideology of modernity, and the critical work of clarifying its supposedly emancipatory effects. To mention but one example, the way in which differences, diversity and singularity are crushed as a result of the beliefs which underlie the acceptance of an essentialist conception of *human nature*, and the universal and, consequently, ahistorical and uniform character that is conferred upon it.

It will be to the extent that anarchism moves away — as has already begun — from the legitimising belief in modernity, that it will find itself in a better position to work towards a weakening of the apparatuses of power, apparatuses set up by it, and, consequently, be better received by those actively opposed to them.

In summary, to enclose utopia in amorous care such that it may shine in all of its splendor; to free it from the weight of its own future visions and hold it in the here and now, we have many paths to tread. We must concentrate our energies on the transformation of the present; materially construct seductive alternatives in the face of what existing society offers us; lock away in the trunk of youthful errors our totalising illusions as nothing more than one option among many; rethink, in depth, our conceptions of power and free ourselves from the vestiges of the legitimising ideology of modernity. These are some of the waystones that seem to point to our current resurgence/renewal of anarchism and they are, I believe, the paths which anarchism will have to pursue, with a firmer step than that which it is taking today, to continue its expansion and deepen its renewal.

ADDENDA

Addendum 1. From modernity to postmodernity

Can the period in which we live, that of the early 21st century, ultimately be located within "modernity"? Or, on the contrary, are there already signs that a radical transformation has begun, sufficient to be considered a new historical epoch?

For the moment this remains unclear. However, I will risk supporting those who believe modernity is still fully in force, but a phase of transition towards another epoch has begun. Perhaps due to a lack of imagination, I'll designate this new vista "postmodernity".

On the one hand, it is obvious that in a period of only a few decades, changes of great magnitude have taken place, as much in the field of technology as in geopolitics and economics, changes that affect the ensemble of society. These changes are not only distinguishable by their magnitude, but by the constant acceleration of the rhythm by which they are produced. The current velocity of the processes of change undoubtedly constitutes an important differentiating factor with respect to the nature of the transformations during earlier centuries.

On the other hand, all epochs produce a legitimating ideology, an ideology that permits its development and acceptance. Modernity does not escape this rule and it also possesses a legitimating ideology which gained form during the Enlightenment and which, perhaps, as a sign of the change of epoch that has already begun, is ceasing to be accepted as the obvious and natural way to contemplate the world, becoming instead an object of radical critiques. But nor does postmodernity escape this rule and it is currently generating its own legitimating ideology through, among other things, a firm opposition to the postulates of modernity.

Let us now briefly examine the characteristics of modernity and postmodernity as historical epochs and as the legitimating ideologies of these epochs.

Modernity as an historical epoch

I understand that modernity is clearly an epoch which has, as with all epochs, a beginning and an end. To speak of "a beginning" should not be taken to mean an isolated, unique moment, but a more or less extensive process of constitution. The reference to "an end" alludes to a period of decline, also more or less extensive, that is a prelude to its exhaustion and the emergence of a new epoch. In effect, modernity does not appear at a precise moment, already equipped with all of its attributes, but rather the distinctive features that shape it constitute themselves progressively over a period of many centuries. Nor will its disappearance be sudden.

The modern epoch began to acquire form in Europe from the beginning of the 15th century, with, among other phenomena, the construction of a new scientific rationality, the decisive invention of the printing press, advances in the arts of navigation or the European discovery of the New World… All the same, it was still necessary to wait some time for the formation of some of its elements, such as the nation state or the declaration of human rights. And it was not until the 18th century, under the Enlightenment, that its legitimating discourse was articulated with a certain clarity.

Modernity is not separable from the constitution of the immense enterprise that "Science" represents, nor from the enormous effects that it has produced on our way of being, our form of life and our form of thinking. Modernity is born together with an ensemble of technological innovations that give rise to a new mode of production, that will slowly configure itself as the capitalist mode of production, giving birth in turn to the process of industrialisation that will accelerate and generalise itself in the later half of the 19th century.

To understand the process of the constitution of modernity, it is worth reviewing for a moment what some researchers, such as Pierre Levy, have called "intelligence technologies". These concern technologies that inscribe themselves in the very process of thought, that have as their function and as effects, rendering possible certain operations of thought that were in no way realisable before these intelligence technologies were constructed; to render possible certain operations of thought, to give them greater efficiency or improve them and, therefore, change them in some sense; to definitively create new forms of thought. Thus writing can be considered an intelligence technology which undoubtedly affected the modalities of thought and had innumerable effects on knowledge. The printing press was another of these intelligence technologies.

The invention of the printing press or, more precisely, its crystallisation and the social diffusion of its use mark the beginnings of modernity. This innovation of intelligence technologies was a crucial element making possible the constitution of modernity, simply because it was fundamental for making possible the constitution of modern scientific reason. Modern scientific knowledge would be practically unthinkable without printed books and all that they imply. The printing press is not only a vector of diffusion and socialisation of knowledge, but it also influences the very form in which it is presented and produced and, therefore, it shapes its very nature. The effect of the printing press goes well beyond the simple facilitation of the circulation of texts. For example, the human subject—author or simple transcriber—is constantly present in the manuscript, even though their presence fades away on the printed page, something that helps to construct the idea of objectivity, so important to modern scientific reason. Graphs, tables, images that are reproduced in multiple copies, without the least difference between them, also contribute to objectifying the representation as something trustworthy, natural and secure, contributing thus to the development of one of the principal constitutive elements of the discourse of modernity, namely: the *ideology of representation.*

As with the printing press in the 15th century, all of the great innovations in the field of intelligence technologies have fundamentally changed societies, such that it is not difficult to understand that when the computer and the electronic processing of information appears in the middle of the 20th century, that this too will produce social effects of the first magnitude.

The ideology of modernity

Despite the considerable heterogeneity of the conceptions and the analyses that forged the world view specific to modernity, it is possible to outline the general features that define it. If Martin Luther's Reformation and Erasmus of Rotterdam's humanism, among others, contributed to constructing its discourse, it was the philosophy of the Enlightenment that gave it body, defining its contents with greater precision. We can synthesise them in the following eleven characteristics:

First, the hyper-valorisation of reason. On the basis of a teleological conception of history, according to which history moves towards a specific end, scientific reason and reason in general appear as vectors of progress and emancipation. History in effect has a point of origin and it progresses in a particular direction that will be appropriate as long as it is always guided by reason. In the process of making reason the central element, definitive of our *I*, according to Descartes, an intrinsic relation, an internal relation between reason and freedom, between reason and progress or between reason and emancipation came to be postulated. From this perspective, the increase of rationality would imply, connaturally, an increase in freedom, and would bring with it the possibility of social progress. Reason is simply emancipatory.

Second, the development of the ideology of representation. That is, among other things, the formulation of knowledge as representation of the world and the subordination of its veracity to the fact that it reproduces reality correctly. This means that knowledge is, in some way, a transcription of the real, a translation of reality to another level — the level of knowledge — that must be as faithful as possible, avoiding any alteration of the translated. The discourse of modernity affirms that this is in fact possible, and thereby automatically establishes a duality, a dichotomy, object-subject, that will drag itself through the whole period of modernity.

A third aspect consists of the attachment to universalism and the belief in the secure foundation of truth. That is, the affirmation according to which the truth — as well as values — can be grounded on indubitable, absolutely true bases. The discourse of modernity is totalising and presents itself as true for all human beings and in all times. This is why the grand narratives, the meta-narratives of modernity, always express themselves in terms of universal values and projects, providing explanations that have an unquestionable, ultimate foundation (for a deeper development of this idea, see the addenda below dedicated to relativism).

Fourth, the affirmation of the centrality of the subject and consciousness. The subject is autonomous, which is to say that in principle it can become the owner or master of itself and the agent of its own history. In like manner, consciousness can be transparent to itself. Important thinkers of modernity concerned themselves with suggesting paths by which consciousness ceases to be an alienated consciousness and comes to be transparent to itself. In this connection, it was Marx who formulated the most genuine social approach regarding what determines consciousness and clouds its transparency.

The fifth aspect concerns the attachment to a humanism based on the belief in the existence of an essential human nature and, more generally, in the adoption of an essentialist perspective. Even though essentialism is not exclusively modern, as it pervades the whole of western philosophy, it is one of the postulates of this ideology most incisively questioned by poststructualism.

Sixth, the figure of the individual was established and individualism as an ideology was fomented. The modern imaginary leads us to think ultimately as individuals who, as such, are all equivalent and who only belong, as if by circumstantial "addition", to specific groups, communities or social categories. In this way, we can move through different communities or distinct social categories, without ever ceasing to be individuals. This signifies that the individual takes the place of the community as the constitutive unit of the social and constitutes itself as the subject of law of modern society.

During the 17th and 18th centuries, John Locke and Jeremy Bentham, among others, elaborated the ingredients of a new moral order that would slowly infiltrate and mould the manner in which we imagine society and our place in it. The principal ideas revolve around the basic notions of social contract, rights and moral obligations of individuals, and mutual self-interest. The basis of these ideas, what legitimates the structures of power that operate in society, is the acceptance of its constituent elements to submit to specific game rules under a sort of founding contract. This is an implicit contract that defines the manner in which the different members of society should behave in relation to each other so as to guarantee their own security and to extract the maximum common benefit. The contract gathers together an ensemble of rights and obligations which the society and the members of the society can demand and must grant to each other mutually.

The novelty is that the social bond is grounded in the rights and the interests of the individuals, such that the obligations imposed by society are justifiable only if they preserve these rights and interests. It is as if the modern individual says to those who govern something like the following:

"I only concede your right to govern me if you do so for my benefit and if you recognise that it is I who conceded it to you ..."

A seventh aspect has to do with the elaboration of the idea of *progress* and the subordination of the present to the future. Modernity is perhaps the first epoch that perceives itself as an epoch; that is, that thinks of itself as a particular moment in a specific process. The moment that an epoch considers itself as such, it is the past that gives meaning to the present. In other words, the current moment can only be understood in reference to the past and it makes the past responsible for the present. This also means that the present is burdened with the responsibility of configuring the future.

The present time transforms itself into a useful time for the future and it has the moral responsibility of assuring that this future be satisfactory. The faith in progress postulates that the present is necessarily better than what was before and worse than what will happen in the future, as long as obstacles are not raised to the correct functioning of reason. The underlying idea here is that the human being can make history, can govern it, instead of being carried by it, leading it in the right direction as long as it allows itself to be guided by reason.

Eighth, modernity is a project and a process of secularisation. The principles and the supreme values upon which is articulated the ideology of society are no longer to be found in the heavens; they abandon transcendence to situate themselves amidst humanity and in the very heart of society. This signifies the metaphorical death of God, understood as the ultimate foundation of the principles upon which society should be based. However, modernity does not leave the place occupied by God empty, but substitutes the figure of a supreme being with other absolute principles, such as universal reason, absolute values or transcendental truth, that tend to have, in practice, the same effects. God disappears, but *its doubles* enter into action. This does not of course take away from the fact that the process of secularisation has important consequences against religious obscurantism, against the arbitrariness of a power that presented itself as the simple executive arm of commands originating elsewhere.

The ninth aspect has to do with fidelity to a secular eschatology and the affirmation of the historicity of societies. Eschatological thought, so important in Christianity, places at the end of time this splendid moment when evil will be definitively defeated; when absolute happiness will be finally attained, when the subject will be fully realised and will leave behind itself a long path of pain and anxieties, finally reconciling itself with itself. Modernity secularised Christian eschatology, emphasising the historicity of our condition and elaborating a series of "grand narratives" about the irrepressible development of progress or the final illumination of all the mysteries of the world, which inspire hope and which promise a kind of final redemption.

This basically means that historicity is our condition. The introduction of historicity into our vision of the world and, thus, into the way in which we conceptualise, represents a substantial change in comparison to other societies. In effect, it assumes that we are no more than a particular moment in a history that has a direction and which advances ineluctably towards a specific end and which, furthermore, will be a happy end. Consequently, hope is fully justified and the great promise borne by the future completely legitimates and renders tolerable all of the suffering that the present may afford us. In this sense, the emancipatory discourses of the 19th century outlined a more or less distant horizon where the conquest of happiness awaits us.

A tenth feature refers to popular sovereignty. Modernity invents "the people" as a new collective agency and establishes popular sovereignty as the source of any pretense to legitimate government. Indeed, it is only possible to govern with the mandate of the people and for the good of the people, and this should give rise to certain means of expression. Some of these are formal and belong specifically to the political sphere, such as for example electoral processes. Others are informal and are found outside this sphere, while conditioning it; it is the case of "public opinion", constructed as a central authority in the political imaginary of modernity.

Lastly, as the eleventh characteristic that should be mentioned, modernity is a process that has slowly led to the development of industrialisation and the "labour enlistment" of the whole population — even though certain sectors, such as women, for example, took considerable time to be integrated into this process. This social innovation, which required the development of a series of apparatuses and techniques, produced multiple consequences. Among them, the centrality conceded to work, the growth of the values associated with it, such as professional conscience and the theorisation of the reasons for which labour and its values should be central elements, even to define our dignity; an ensemble of elements that have continued to diminish in the present, which perhaps signals the incipient exhaustion of the modern epoch.

Let us not however precipitate ourselves. Modernity reached one of its most complete expressions in a very recent epoch, as recent as the 1950's, with the process of *modernisation* (the very term "modernisation" is relatively recent). Modernisation appeared as one of the principal political values for those who govern, as that which populations should pursue and what countries should realise. It is a matter of increasing, as much as is possible, the rationalisation of the economy and society. Its discourse is formulated in terms such as "raising the per capita income of countries", "maximising the development of productive forces", "increasing productivity", "expanding the capacity and mobility of available resources", "improving competitiveness", "increasing purchasing power", etc.

On the political level, modernity has endeavoured to generalise the democratic model of political participation, considered as the form of political functioning most adequate to making possible the process of modernisation and drawing out all of its benefits.

In addition to having propitiated certain social advances, modernity has had some very significant costs. It was necessary to pay a very high price for its very development, resulting in an enormous quantity of suffering for the victims of the process, that is, for all of those elements considered marginal with respect to the fundamental values of modernity, for everyone who was in a peripheral position with respect to the centres of power of modernity, and for all of those parts of the world which were colonised so that modernity could prosper and strengthen itself.

Postmodernity as a historical epoch

In the same way that the Modern Epoch began with a series of technical innovations, such as the printing press, postmodernity also began with an important technological innovation, the electronic processing of information. The power and speed that information technologies have introduced into the treatment and generation of information are not only at the basis of the *knowledge society*, they have also provoked the exponential development of communications, the acceleration of the process of globalisation, the establishment of *a new economic order* and the upsurge of biotechnologies, which, thanks to genetic engineering, have opened up the possibility of artificially selecting certain human characteristics. The simultaneous development, beginning in the 1990's, of cyberspace, a network of electronic interconnections, has had a decisive bearing on all facets of the social fabric; relationally, economically, politically, symbolically, and so on.

In view of these elements, it is easy to understand that the transforming impact of the computer in areas such as production, work, commerce or science, are configuring new conditions of life and a new social framework which cannot but change our vision of the world.

Zygmunt Bauman, the sociologist, who prefers to speak of "liquid modernity" instead of "postmodernity", captures with acuity some of the most significant aspects of the new social reality that is forming. To address but one: Acceleration, in all areas, constitutes one of the defining features of a new epoch where everything flows at a vertiginous rhythm. Thus, for example, the obsolescence of products, that until recently was a defect against which one had to struggle—duration was sold—has ceased to be a problem. Today, the speed of becoming obsolete has turned into an advantage for goods: everything ages with enormous velocity and must be quickly substituted. This programmed obsolescence and the necessity of change affects not not only industrial products, but extends to all of the phenomena of the work world and daily life: contracts are unstable, commitments are ephemeral. A permanent disposition to change must be manifest, changing direction with each little sign, seeking to be free of any long term ties and maintaining a flexible identity in a world of fluid and momentary connections.

All of these transformations, to which can be added the constant relocations, the reduction of the life cycles of the skills demanded of workers, the deregulation of labour relations, etc., daily feed the feeling of unpredictability and insecurity before the future. The idea that no one will exercise a single, unique profession, nor that they will dispose of the same employment for life, is consolidated and generalised; in the same way that no one is guaranteed the possibility of always remaining in the same place.

The perspective of professional migration, of territorial migration, of skills migration and the uncertainty of payment, sustain an imaginary where lasting, stable identities and, furthermore, permanent identities shaped on the basis of work, cease to be meaningful. This announces the end, therefore, not of work, but of the peculiar ideology of work which was so important in the last phase of modernity. And the end, also, of what we could call identity sedentariness, substituted by the perspective of identity nomadism.

The ideology of postmodernity

Two centuries had to pass, since the beginnings of modernity, for the conditions to be present for the elaboration of the legitimising discourse of this epoch and to gain awareness that it was effectively "an epoch". Two centuries in addition to the three or four decades that separate us from the beginning of postmodernity. Even taking into account the strong acceleration of historical and social time, the brevity of the time that has passed explains the confusing, diverse, contradictory, incoherent and fragmentary nature of the legitimising discourse of postmodernity.

In fact, the discourse of postmodernity presents a double aspect: it develops, first, a powerful criticism of the ideological presuppositions of modernity — in this sense, postmodernity is an anti-modernity — and it elaborates, secondly, the bases of a legitimising discourse for the new epoch.

While critical of the ideology of modernity, postmodern discourse invites us to see reason, presented as emancipatory, as having in practice totalitarian type consequences. In effect, reason constitutes, among other things, an apparatus of annihilation of differences, however not of differences in terms of inequalities, but of the diversity and the singularities which manifest themselves in all domains, including in the domain of cultures. Reason orders, classifies, universalises, unifies and, for this, it must reduce, expel, neutralise and suppress differences. As well, in its programmatic discourse, modernity promised social progress and wise dominion of nature, but these commitments were not fulfilled. Auschwitz, Hiroshima, the depletion of the planet's resources and the destruction of minority cultures are some of the consequences brought about by the modern pretension of converting ourselves into the owners and possessors of nature.

The great principles of modernity are, according to postmodern discourse, nothing but simple stories told to legitimate an epoch. The grand narratives are deceiving narratives that hide the enormous effects of power. Behind the beautiful declarations about the autonomy of the subject and about the self-transparency of consciousness, stalked practices of subjection. Truth, objectivity and the secure foundations of knowledge in fact hid particular values disguised behind the pretensions of neutrality, objectivity and universality. Indeed, modernity is not reproached for having killed God, but for having put in the place of absolutes rooted in the heavens, new absolutes that produced the same effects in a more cunning manner.

Considering now the second aspect of postmodern ideology, we see that the effort to elaborate the legitimising bases of the new epoch insists on the fragmentation of reality, of the subject, and also on relativism in the field of knowledge and values.

In the new ideological scenario, eschatology is weakening, the grand emancipatory narratives no longer seduce the imagination, and the horizon of hope that these drew and the great promise that they sheltered ceased to be believable. The perspective of a distant, but secure, goal, outlined by science, in terms of progress, or by politics, in terms of the end of exploitation and domination, is no longer satisfactory. The lines that sketched the path towards emancipation lost clarity, giving way to the idea that there is no pre-established path, no map that could safely direct the navigation towards a future of freedom and happiness. And all of this translates into a strong scepticism and towards a rejection of any *long-term project*, whether of a political nature, or existential.

The feeling that the present should not be mortgaged to what the future may bring us has continued to increase and that we should live in the present instant against what some eventual better future has ceased to guarantee. Presentism, the desire to extract all that is possible from the present and to consume the instant, substitutes the sacrifice of investing for tomorrow. Precarious ways of life install themselves in the ephemeral, the immediate is what truly counts, because no hopeful future is guaranteed, and thus the idea that there *is no future* continues to gain strength.

The secularisation driven by modernity grounded itself in the conviction that our historicity propelled us necessarily towards a future of progress, sought after through the rationality of human actions. However, in those moments in which the conviction falters, when the future becomes uncertain and uncontrollable and when eschatology weakens, it seems that secularisation leaves us overly unprotected and that it is necessary to search for protecting transcendent realities which offer us security. We are accordingly witness to a certain return of religious sentiment, the proliferation of sects and esoteric groups, and a greater acceptance of the supernatural and of mysteries that refer to magical thought. It is perhaps for this reason that the ideology of the new times encourages the abandonment of a strict rationality, thereby weakening the border between facts and values, between the affective and the cognitive, or between the real and the virtual.

Perhaps it is also for this reason that *the event* exercises, currently, such an intense fascination on people. Resistant to historicity, the event is what cannot be predicted, what breaks with the logic of rational expectations and represents one of the highest expressions of discontinuity. There is no doubt that there is, currently, an enormous desire for events, a desire for exceptional incidents, even if they are catastrophic, a collective appetite for that which surprises, is unique and which occurs without previous warning. Populations are hungry for events. Perhaps, however, this is also a revenge against power, a kind of compensation for the feeling that everything is under control, a sort of challenge to a power that appears to be able to do everything, except, by definition, to predict an event, given that this would cease to be an event if it were predictable.

Before the ideal of a self-possessed individual, constituted as the supporting and legitimating unity of society, the desire of group fusion and intersubjective valorisation gains form. A tendency towards tribal identifications manifests itself. A necessity for strong identifications which certainly promote practices of solidarity and mutual aid, but which at the same time confine them to the interior spaces of the groups to which one belongs. The desire to fuse into the community and to dissolve oneself in the collective outlines a project that exhausts itself in the mere satisfaction of *being together*.

Despite the fact that people continue to mobilise in the streets and continue to participate in elections, symptoms of a global lack of concern for the political sphere are discernible. Scepticism gains ground and increases the distance between political representatives and those represented. After having been a key element in the political imaginary of modernity, public opinion not only appears as infinitely fragmented, but is also ever more perceived as powerfully instrumentalised by the communications media and by the powers which control them. It is obvious that if public opinion is constructed through power, it can no longer serve as an alibi to legitimate it and to have us believe that power respects the public will. Consequently, the problem that political power must now confront is that people desert it and that they neither desire to commit themselves to it nor to participate in it, limiting themselves to living in its shadow and abandoning it completely to the hands of those who manage it.

To conclude these considerations on the epoch that is beginning to emerge, I want to emphasise that, as modernity established new forms of domination, so too is postmodernity doing the same. To be convinced of this, one has but to think of the effects that social networks have on our ways of being and on how we relate to each other, or of the surveillance that ICTs make possible, or also the kind of governmentality that the medicalisation of life puts into practice. Therefore, it is by no means a matter of completely celebrating the entrance into postmodernity. What is to be thanked is the demystification and critique of modernity, a critique that, if it serves anything, makes us more sensitive to the effects of domination generated by the grand principles of modernity and to which we submitted without even knowing that we were doing so.

Should we mobilise ourselves against postmodernity? I believe that yes, but of course, not in the name of modernity … Should we turn away from the discourse of postmodernity? I believe not. To ignore it, to not wish to listen to it, to not want to understand it, is an enormous hoax, for as we reject the name, the thing continues to advance. Our subjectivity, our ways of subjectification, our closest reality, our social environment … all of this, whether we want it or not, whether we accept postmodernity or not, is changing. The still confused discourse of postmodernity must be studied and analysed seriously, as much to better understand the modernity which has constituted us and which has shaped our way of thinking, as to try to see the nature of newly approaching forms of domination. If we want to understand the present and strengthen our capacity for action, then we must decipher the discourse of postmodernity.

Addendum 2. Post-structuralism as a turning point in ways of thinking

The influence of post-structuralism on the configuration of postanarchism is of such a magnitude that to gain a proper understanding of the latter, it is useful to examine it with care. Before we stop to consider three aspects — the question of the subject, the essentialist postulate and the problematic of power — which are of special relevance to rethink anarchism and which occupy a privileged place in the current of postanarchism, it is necessary to situate the immediate predecessor of post-structuralism, that is, structuralism.

Structuralism

Structuralism is a cultural movement that gestated in the early 1950's. It affirmed itself throughout the same decade (1955, the year Claude

Levi-Strauss' *Tristes Tropiques* was published, was emblematic) and consolidated itself in the decade of the 60's. The apogee of the movement was possibly reached in 1966, a year baptised in France as "the structuralist year". Structuralism's decline however began in this same decade, in the wake of the critical impact of May '68. It nevertheless continued to shine until the mid-1970's, giving way at that moment to post-structuralism.

Structuralism took some of its principal conceptual tools from Ferdinand de Saussure, founder of modern linguistics. For Saussure, the sign, the constitutive unit of language, has no importance in itself, it lacks positive significance. Its significance does not result from its content but from its position, from the place that it occupies with respect to all of the other signs, that is, from the difference that it maintains with respect to other signs. This means that we should not concentrate on the terms that are in relation to each other, but on the relationships between these terms. In this manner, specific contents are excluded, the signifier is privileged over the signified, the code over the message, which is to say, essentially, the formal structure of the language is privileged over the circumstantial statements that can be produced by means of it.

Saussure also emphasised the dichotomy between language and speech. Speech is but one manifestation, one realisation, one particular expression determined by language, by the code. This means that to understand the system of a language, we have to set aside its circumstantial manifestations, we have to ignore speech. Linguistics constitutes itself whileexcluding the one who speaks, pushing away the subject.

The dichotomy between synchrony and diachrony also reveals itself to be crucial and the metaphor of chess helps us to capture its meaning. In effect, Saussure says that to take a decision in playing chess, what is important are the positions occupied by the chess pieces on the board, their differential value and the possible combinations between the pieces. How this situation was arrived at — that is, the history that led to this particular arrangement on the board — may be interesting, but, at the time of deciding, it is purely anecdotal. What else does the path along which we arrived at this situation give? It is the configuration of the situation which conditions our decision. It is therefore necessary to analyse the structure as such; the way in which this structure arranged itself is of no concern. And this means that history must be excluded from our preoccupations.

Structuralism thus excluded a series of dimensions that had hitherto seemed important, such as the referent, contents, the subject, history.

On the level of philosophy, structuralism constituted itself in opposition to phenomenology and, more generally, against the philosophy of consciousness.

Phenomenology places the accent on the experiential, on the directly lived, on subjectivity as the constituent element of our experience of things and of ourselves. According to phenomenology, the world is transparent to the consciousness of the subject, provided that consciousness frees itself from everything that constrains and distorts it. The subject's consciousness is also transparent to itself, as long as the necessary precautions are taken. For example, it is obvious that an alienated consciousness cannot be transparent to itself. Phenomenology places at the forefront the conscious subject, the consciousness of the subject and the power of consciousness. This means that knowledge involves the rigorous questioning of the subject's consciousness.

Structuralism constitutes itself precisely against these presuppositions and sustains that consciousness is opaque to itself, that the subject and consciousness are not constituent, but rather constituted. They are constituted by language, by codes, by structures, by culture, by the unconscious ... Accordingly, it is useless to interrogate the consciousness of the subject. What must be questioned is what speaks in and through the subject without the latter being conscious of it. And, consequently, the subject must be radically eliminated, the subject of modernity, of phenomenology, the subject as transparent consciousness of itself.

What must be sought out is what hides behind experience and what renders it possible; to investigate what, lying behind appearances, engenders the manifest and the visible. One has to go behind the facts to see what produces them; one therefore has to search for the latent and invisible structures. The truth hides behind what can be seen, lying in the depths covered over by appearances. The metaphor of the researcher is that of the diver.

Structuralism shares some of the fundamental presuppositions of modernity. It values scientificity and gives therefore a privileged place to reason—and to scientific reason in particular—it assumes a certain essentialism and a certain belief in human nature; it participates in the search for universals, etc.

It nonetheless also questions some of the basic presuppositions of modernity. Concretely, it rejects the idea of an autonomous subject, of a subject creator of itself of itself and of history, and shares in the criticism of the subject as a consciousness transparent to itself.

May '68 and the decline of structuralism

Structuralism acquired an enormous influence in the heart of the cultural and intellectual world. It was however when it found itself at the apogee of its recognition, marking the thought of an entire epoch, that something surged forth that no one could predict—and even less the structuralists: the eruption of May '68 and this was lethal for structuralism.

In the first place, May '68 was an *event* and, as such, something that structuralism rejected, in principle, as secondary and insignificant. The psychoanalyst Jacques Lacan sought to play down the importance of the graffiti, the demonstrations and the street disturbances, saying: nothing important will happen because "structures do not fill the streets". Later, before the magnitude of the event, Lacan sought to correct matters saying that "it was the structures that filled the streets". Lacan however doubly equivocated: what was happening was important, and it was not structures that were in the streets, it was *subjects*.

In the same way, May '68 also put into question totalising, globalising and universalising discourses, legitimating the local, the particular and the specific. This contestation could not but affect structuralism, given that it raised suspicion against a type of discourse that corresponded effectively with what it maintained.

Post-structuralism

May '68 strengthened the conditions for the implosion of structuralism and activated the time bomb that destabilised it and made way for post-structuralism. This latter was constituted on the basis of a denunciation of the former's *impasses* and its acritical assumption of many of the presuppositions of modernity. Structuralism, for example, is questioned on the grounds that it takes for granted the universal character of scientific reason, accepting concepts such as the truth, certainty or objectivity, and that it seeks to ground knowledge on absolute and definitive foundations.

The humanism that beats in structuralism is also questioned. In effect, despite the fact that it advocated the elimination of the subject, its search for the invariable, for universals and transcultural constants, which are neither historical nor contingent, evidences a profound essentialism that joins with the belief in the existence of *human nature*.

Post-structuralism manifests a radical disagreement with structuralist ahistoricism. The exclusion of history is considered inadmissible and Foucault played an important role in this critique. Nevertheless, when post-structuralism reintegrates history and introduces movement to structures—giving to them their genesis and their dynamism - it does not take up the concept of history specific to modernity. It rejects history as continuity, history as something with a direction and that advances progressively towards specific goals that always improve upon earlier ones. The post-structuralist conception of history is different, it is discontinuous, lacks any end or purpose and is not evolutionist. It is a historicised structuralism that is characterised by the re-introduction of history into the heart of structure.

Lastly, the exclusion of the subject is also questioned. The subject reappeared in an indirect way as a consequence of the consideration of non-discursive practices which form part of what is outside a text. It also appeared in a direct way as a result of the importance covered by *enunciation* and, therefore, the necessity of taking into account the spoken. In this manner, the subject re-integrates itself in structures, it is again present in them, but no longer as the former subject, not as the subject of modernity; it is not an instituting subject. It is a subject already constituted, but which still plays an active role.

What remains of structuralism in post-structuralism is, almost exclusively, the critique of phenomenology and the categorical rejection of the *conscious subject* of modernity.

Essentialism

Post-structuralism is characterised by its radical rejection of the essentialist perspectives that have accompanied a considerable part of philosophy since Antiquity and that pervade the ideology of modernity.

If the existence of being — of any kind of being — is always a concrete and situated existence that occurs in *a particular world*, then it is inevitable that the changing characteristics of this world condition and mould the concrete expressions of this *being*. The essentialist postulate however pretends that independently of the social and historical conditionalities which it may have suffered, *being*, endowed with a constitutive essence, remains fundamentally *the same*. Behind the contingent and variable modalities of being, as and how it manifests itself, there consequently exists a fixed and invariable, essential being.

Thus beneath the changing forms of that which represses it, is found our constitutive desire; beneath the fluctuating regimes of truth and the sinuous trajectory of reason, is found the truth in its unalterableness and rationality in itself; or beneath the extensive cultural, social and historical diversity which subjects present, is found invariable *human nature.*

Essentialism takes us back directly to the game thought up by Plato which consists in turning our eyes away from the deceitful shadows that surround us, so as to thereby accede to the essence of things, the unalterable and eternal truth of their being, well beyond the circumstantial distortions imposed by existence.

Accordingly, essentialism incites us to bring together, as much as possible, an existence with the essence that grounds it. Beyond that which appears to us to be, or that which the vicissitudes of our existence have led us to be, what we *are*, authentically, is a consequence of *what is already inscribed in our essence.* Consequently, we should *rediscover* this essence which lies beneath what obscures and deforms it, so as to *attach* ourselves to it as much as it is possible and, thereby, fully *realise ourselves.* It is necessary to break with the distance that separates us from our *true self,* from *authentic* reason, from the constitutive *nature* of the human being, because it is in this same distance that is rooted precisely our infelicity and our alienation, our difficulty in realising ourselves fully or in acceding to the full truth. In sum, to find a happiness that is born of the coincidence between what we truly are and what we appear to be, it is clear that we have to endeavour to be *faithful* to our own essence.

Furthermore, in considering that existence is no more than the simple, temporary manifestation of the essence that sustains it, it follows that essentialism emphatically denies the possibility of *creating* and closes down the very possibility of freedom. In effect, as Castoriadis said, *to create*, in the strong sense of the term, is to produce something that is not already fully contained in what is given, in what already exists up to this moment. Accordingly, if what already exists is "the changeable expression of an immutable essence", whatever we can produce will only represent an expression, distinct as regards form, of this unchanging essence. If things have *an essence*, our practices cannot create anything that is not already part of it. This marks the strict limit of our freedom, a freedom which can only transform, but which can never reach radical novelty.

Following Foucault, one of the principal elements that characterise post-structuralism is the desire to *contradict the essentialist postulate*. It is a matter of neutralising its implications and of demonstrating not only that it is an *intellectual fallacy*, but that it represents, in addition, *a dangerous fallacy* for the exercise of our freedom. Behind the *being that is*, that is, of the being that truly exists, there is not *its true being* which we could reach by cleansing it of its contingent and accidental aspects, which cover its real existence. *Essence is subsumed in existence*, it does not exist as something separate from it—simply put, *it does not exist*—and thus to search for it is completely vain. *Essence* is a useless, erroneous and deceitful concept and that is consequently dangerous for our practices of freedom. We only possess *existence*, with its irremediably contingent character.

The subject

One of the elements that best defines post-structuralism is its reformulation of the question of the subject. It not only reintroduces the subject where structuralism had eliminated it, but it also dismantles the essentialist conception of the subject inherited from modernity.

The philosopher Richard Rorty belongs to those who question the idea according to which people are constituted, in the depths of their being, by a *true I*, by an essential and immutable *human nature*, that had been repressed and covered over by historical institutions and practices. There is, according to Rorty, no *intrinsic human nature* that we could rescue, that we could *free from alienation* or that we have to go on progressively *realising* so as to *finally find ourselves*, as we *really* are.

There is no project for the human being that we might elaborate that would be legitimated by the claim that it is closer than others to its true nature, or that it is more in conformity than others with what is truly the case and which would allow for *a more complete form of self-realisation.*

Of course, we can elaborate transformative projects and we can *desire to be differently,* ceasing to be what we are today, but we must argue for these projects with justifications that make no appeal to our supposed essence. We can, for example, want to be more free, but not because freedom constitutes an exigency inscribed in our nature, nor because it is an exigency that we want to satisfy so as to be, thereby, more *fully human.*

We may want to construct ourselves one way or the other, but none of these ways will be more or less in conformity with our true nature; simply because there is no such thing.

Obviously and fortunately, we can come to be different from what circumstances have made us out to be because we can *create* ourselves in another way.

Foucault, following Nietzsche on the *de-subjectification of the subject,* shelved the category of the subject as a transhistorical element, the ground of experience, and radically inverted the basic assumptions of phenomenology. It is not the subject that is the condition for the possibility of experience, but rather, *it is experience that constitutes the subject.* Or, instead, it is experience that constitutes the plurality of subjects that inhabit the subject-form. It follows, consequently, that the subject, far from being a universal, transhistorical and foundational being, is but a *changing historical product,* as variable as experience itself may be.

In other words, the subject is always the result of specific *practices of subjectification,* historically situated, which need to be analysed if we wish to know how we came to be what we are. It is on this basis that eventually we can act so as to cease to be who we are, to think differently, to create other things, to feel distinctly, to desire in a different way and establish other values. Things neither necessarily have to be as they are—however difficult it is to imagine that they can be different — nor do we have to be as we are — however difficult it is to discern the very path of a possible alternative.

Power

Post-structuralism, above all in its Foucaldian version, distinguishes itself by the incisive re-conceptualisation of the question of power. According to Foucault, power must not be thought of as exclusively under the form of the law, the State, political authority, as what constrains our freedom, as what prohibits or sanctions our transgressions. Or rather, power is effectively all of this, but it is not only this. The error we usually make consists in *taking the part for the whole*, by reducing power to a single modality. Foucault does the opposite. He puts into parenthesis power's most visible form, not to say the only form that is clearly visible, and centres his attention on the other diverse and multiple forms of the exercise of power, which were able to develop widely because they hid themselves from our sight.

According to Foucault, power is not a thing, it is not a property, it is not something which characterises specific entities, it is not something which is possessed or owned, but is *a relationship*; it is not something which is in a particular place, clearly located. Power is not something which descends — the traditional image — power ascends; it is not something which pervades everything from above and which continues to irradiate and penetrate everywhere, controlling everything. Power is created and sprouts forth from all spheres of the social because it is immanent to it.

Through a very complex play of the constitution of an *ensemble of effects*, the distinct forms of power that emerge in different social fields reciprocally feed each other, to converge in large tendencies which initiate ascending movements and contribute to configuring the State and the centres of power.

Thus the form of the State is not independent of the relationships of power which are generated, which are woven, in the social fabric. Power *above*—the State and centres of power—is constituted in part, also, by what comes from *below*. However, from these centres and from the State, the exercise of power also flows and projects itself below, eliminating or, on the contrary, selecting and animating the relations of power that are forged there. It is obvious that to speak of an ascending power does not signify, far from it, that the power of the State is underestimated.

Power not only functions according to the model of the law, it also functions under the model of *the norm* and it is, basically, normalising. While the law is prescriptive, the norm is simply declarative, not only expressing a legitimised knowledge that tells us what *we have* to do, but also what it would be *normal* to do. It does not oblige us to be a specific way, but rather informs us of how the majority of our fellows are; and if, in comparing ourselves with them, it follows that we are not as we ought to be, then we endeavour to eliminate or reduce this difference so as to be *normal*. It is evident that the norm, and the process of normalisation, does not function like the law. The latter always needs a sanctioning mechanism, while the former only requires a prompting mechanism that can push us towards a greater conformity. On the other hand, power is not principally a negative authority which limits and constrains. Power is basically *productive*; it is in part constitutive of desire, freedom, and the subject. This means that it is already present in these elements and that there is not, therefore, a possible exteriority to relations of power.

However, if power is a relation and, more precisely, a relation of forces, then where there is power there is also necessarily resistance. Power implies, ineluctably, resistance, for the mere fact that it constitutes itself within a relation of forces between things that are in confrontation. Let us not though celebrate this fact too quickly. This resistance is not in a relation of exteriority with respect to power, it remains within its fabric, it is one of its components and shares with it far more than we usually imagine. Even knowing that it does not represent a radical alterity to power, it is, for Foucault, a matter of multiplying the lines of resistance as lines of intervention by power are deployed. The resonances and the imbrications between resistances and power mean that there is neither a discourse nor a practice that is intrinsically liberating. This or that discourse, this or that practice, may constitute resistance to power in a specific moment, but not because they are intrinsically emancipating or liberating. We must suspect any discourse that pretends to be intrinsically liberating, for it is with this, precisely, that the danger begins.

I cannot resist including a long quotation from Michel Foucault to conclude these quick annotations on a conception of power that has been adopted by post-structuralism and, to a large extent, by postanarchism. In his last interview, just a few days before dying, Foucault said:

> *… what we can also observe is that there can be no relations of power unless subjects are free [...] To exercise a relation of power, a certain form of freedom has to be present. This means that in relations of power, there necessarily has to be the possibility of resistance, for if there were no possibility of resistance—a violent type of resistance, resistance as flight, astute resistance, of strategies to change this situation, to modify it -, then there would be no relations of power. Given that this is how I approach the matter, I refuse to answer this question that I am so often asked: "if power is everywhere, then there is no freedom?" [...] If there are relations of power throughout society, it is because there is freedom everywhere.*

Addendum 3. Relativism against absolutism: truth and ethics

For many reasons, relativism merits considerable attention from our part. Firstly, because as it radically rejects some of the more questionable presuppositions of the ideology of the Enlightenment, it displays clear affinities with post-structuralism and postmodernism and consequently finds itself quite close to the kind of thought that inspires postanarchism.

It follows, furthermore, that as relativism undermines, by the same root, the principle of authority and radically questions every absolutist argument, that it is disposed to bring a greater flow of water to the anarchist mill than any other current of philosophy. This is even more so as it proffers tools to anarchism to make evident and neutralise traces of authoritarian principles that modern thought may have left in its midst.

There is still however a third argument for relativism which motivates our particular attention. It has to do with the extraordinary hostility shown towards it and the merciless ostracism to which it has been subject; "Vade retro Satanás" ["Step back, Satan"] has been, it might be said, the anti-relativist *leitmotiv*. In effect, relativist disqualifications and the blunt *anathemas* directed against relativist positions constitute a historical constant. We find these disqualifications in Plato, when he ridicules Protagoras; and we find it as well in the famous encyclical of John Paul II, published in 1993 and entitled *Veritati Spendor*, wherein it is proclaimed that the relativist questioning of truth is one of the worst threats that looms over humanity. A warning that, two days before becoming Benedict XVI, cardinal Ratzinger reaffirmed with vehemence in the homily of the mass *Pro Eligendo Pontifice*. In fact, it is quite frequent to hear conservative voices putting us seriously on guard against the devastating effects which relativism has on the moral values of our civilisation. But it is no less frequent to hear progressive voices proclaim that relativism is dangerous, even for simple peaceful and civilised coexistence, given that it would lead us in the end to accept brute force as the ultimate means to settle our differences.

The fears which relativism gives rise to evoke those that *the death of God* caused among people some decades ago: "if God is dead, then all is permitted", "the law of the jungle will impose itself", "man will become a wolf to man", and other nonsense of the same kind. We know that it was precisely *the idea of God* which disguised the masked reign of the law of the jungle and that the abandonment of this idea does not end at an *ethical precipice*, on the contrary. And nor does the death of the truth and the farewell to universal principles lead to ethical catastrophes. It was precisely the respect for the divinity and the invocation of these grand principles that blocked the very possibility of an ethics.

This hostility is perfectly understandable when it comes from religious sectors, given that theistic belief demands *the absolute*, for obvious reasons. Faith may experience moments of doubt and stagger momentarily, but it is not fully itself except in absolute certainty. If one has faith, then God *truly* exists and exists for everyone since the beginning of time and forever; including for those who deny its existence. The relativist is therefore seen as an abominable *unbeliever*, given that they question, in principle, all universals. Curiously, this same hostility also originates with those who defend that *scientific reason* transcends, necessarily, socio-historical circumstances and that it situates itself in the absolute. To the extent that they question the universality of scientific reason, the relativist is seen consequently as a dangerous *obscurantist*.

Given this so generalised and intense hostility, relativism is condemned and rejected, more often than not, without even bothering to have a quick look at its arguments. In effect, it is as if since the time of Plato the issue has been resolved once and for all and that nobody with any sense could do anything but energetically distance themselves from it.

It is a simple question of logic: if, as relativism maintains, truth does not exist, then neither can it be true that the truth does not exist. Therefore, the affirmation "the truth does not exist" is not true; and if it is not, then it is true that "the truth exists" and relativism is consequently false. The argument from self-contradiction deals a mortal blow that seems to bring to a definitive conclusion any discussion.

Nonetheless, instead of reassuring us, it is the very bluntness of the argument of self-refutation that should provoke suspicion. For if things are as clear as they appear to be, if relativism is such a foolish, ridiculous, inconsistent and unsustainable position, as Plato affirmed, it would have been logical for the question of relativism to have been closed at the very moment of its formulation. How can it be explained, then, that rather than passing away, it has remained alive for centuries, that it has reached our own days and has even experienced a spectacular *boom* in the last decades?

It is very easy to show, as we will see further on, that the supposed self-contradiction, into which relativism falls, disappears as soon as we cease to play the game established by the absolutists. This is a game that sets up, as an imperative condition to start a discussion about the truth, that the discussion obey the argumentative rules established by the absolutist conception of truth. It is a matter then of a game that consists of using the criterion that is itself under discussion, namely: the truth, as an argument to settle precisely the discussion about this criterion.

It is evident that if it is demanded of the relativist that they affirm the truth of their affirmations, they cannot but fall into contradiction, given that it is the very criterion of truth that they dispute. It cannot be asked of someone who rejects the concept of truth whether what they say is true or false. They should rather be asked what reasons they have for believing that their position is better or whicharguments make it more acceptable than another. The relativist only falls into self-contradiction when they claim for themself what they deny to others. However, in that case, not only is the relativist self-contradictory, but they also become an anti-relativist.

We can also see that, repeating the strategy that consists of enclosing relativism in a spiral of self-contradictions, the absolutists make it affirm that "all points of view are equivalent, and no one view is better or truer than any other". This assertion would oblige the relativist to place themself in the absurd situation of having to present their view, immediately admitting that there is no good reason for considering it better than any other point of view and that no one, not even the relativist themself, have any motive to prefer it to anything else. Of course, as we will see shortly, relativism does not have to accept anything like the affirmation that there are no points of view which are not preferable to others.

It is because I am fully convinced that relativism provides tools of the highest quality to develop practices of freedom and because it does not appear to me to be correct that a millenarian tradition of disqualification should have succeeded in condemning it without due process, that it seems to me important to contribute to dissipating some of the errors that surround its image and to advocate here in its favour.

The ethical question

It is precisely on the terrain of ethics where it is usual to say that relativism constitutes the worst of all possible options. In effect, it is accused, among many other things, of dissolving moral values by affirming that all values are equal; of promoting ethical indifference by sustaining that nothing justifies ethical commitment; and of opening the door to the law of the jungle by allowing for nothing else but the use of force as the final resort to settle disagreements. These three accusations are sufficiently grave to have us ask whether they have any kind of foundation.

However, in the first place, the relativist does not affirm that all ethical options are equivalent and that no one option is better or worse than any other.

What the relativist in fact defends is that any moral option is as good as any other and that all ethical values are strictly equivalent, but only *from the perspective of their ultimate foundation*. It is from the point of view of the common absence of an ultimate foundation that the relativist traces a strict equivalence among all ethical values. It is the case that if the relativist had to turn to the criterion of the foundation or the objectivity of values to establish which are better, that they could only abstain from any choice, declaring them all equivalent. Nevertheless, what characterises relativism is precisely the categorical rejection of the criterion of ultimate foundation to discriminate between values. With the result that nothing obliges them to affirm that there are no values that are not superior to others.

From the affirmation according to which there are no values that are *objectively* better than others because all of them lack an ultimate foundation, the affirmation cannot be inferred according to which it is not possible to differentiate between values.

Therefore, a relativist can state, without contradiction, that their values are *better* than others, that certain *forms of life* are preferable to others and that they are eventually prepared to struggle for them. However, in contrast to the absolutist, they declare at the same time that these values which they assume as *better* lack any ultimate foundation, being, in this respect, *equivalent* to any other value.

In contrast to the absolutist, a relativist cannot argue against a Nazi on the basis that the values that the latter defends are *objectively* reprehensible or that the practices that this same approves of transgress unquestionable moral norms. They can only counter their own values and present the reasons that they have to defend them, but without claiming a privileged status for them against those who question them.

With regards to the second accusation, relativism in fact does not defend that nothing can justify ethical commitment and that it is all the same whether one sets out to defend certain ideas or remains quietly at home watching a soap opera.

For what reason would we only be justified in defending our values on the condition that they be assumed to be absolute and universal? To affirm that these depend on us, that they are relative to our practices and our decisions, is to assume that they stand only by the activity that we deploy to defend them. In the absence of any transcendent principle to establish the hierarchy of values, to make a determined normative choice obliges the person who makes it to defend the choice with all possible vigour, given that they know that *it rests upon nothing more than the defence, argumentative or of another kind, that is capable of unfolding it*, and that the full responsibility for the choice made falls entirely upon them.

It is precisely because they do not feel themself pushed by any imperative necessity in the choice of their normative commitments that the relativist is far from, if not to say at the opposite pole of, a supposed moral indifference.

It is when values are postulated as absolute, it is when they *depend on nothing* and, above all, when they do not depend on ourselves, that then defending them becomes secondary. In forming part of an order which is not susceptible to change, for in such a case, it would not be absolute, then its adoption simply testifies that *we submit* to the imperatives traced by the straight path of the *Good* and of *Truth*. To accept a system of values which, in not depending on ourselves, only offers us the possibility of acceptance, leads us to the abandonment of any critical thought and to the renunciation of any attempt to exercise our freedom.

Inhibition and de-mobilisation result when it is believed, as the absolutist does, that values *exist* anyway and that, to the extent that they are *objective*, they will exist *in secula seculorum*; whether we do anything for this to be the case, or not. It is precisely when one believes in the transcendence of values when it becomes secondary and dispensable to defend them or not. Furthermore, good consciousness, the tranquility of the spirit and the absence of any trace of doubt, constitute the legacy of someone who knows that when they act according to the *Moral law*, that they do not have to give an account of their actions because these do not refer to one's responsibility, but to what has been dictated by authorities which surpass them and which do not depend on them.

Accordingly, for example, no absolute moral imperative obliges us to struggle against privileges and injustices. It concerns a decision that is taken or not, influenced by circumstances. As with an absolutist, a relativist can take this decision or not, but if they take it, then they cannot find encouragement in the idea that they are supported by universal principles which indicate the path to the *Good* and the *Truth*. They will limit themselves to saying that this struggle constitutes *their* particular option and will try to argue in defence of this option without appealing to *anything* that transcends it.

The third reproach against relativism is that it opens the path to the law of the jungle. However, it still has to be seen if relativism appeals to force as the final argument to resolve differences.

The answer is *yes*. When all of the arguments are exhausted, nothing remains but relations of force. The relativist nevertheless asks: what is the difference that separates them from the absolutist, on this point?

And the response is … that *there is not the least difference*.

In effect, even though the absolutist presents theirs own position as what permits the use of force to be avoided, they cannot hide that they also resort to it as the ultimate argument to settle the differences with those who do not assume their rules of play and *refuse to be reasonable*. However, they do this furthermore with the aggravating circumstance which consists in stigmatising the victim of this violence.

To the extent that, as the absolutist contends, ethical criteria do not depend on our decisions and possess an *objective* value, it is obvious that to not accept these criteria can only be a mistake or a demonstration of irrationality. If we reject what has been *objectively* established as *morally* good, it is because we are in no way normal, because we are perverse. This *perversion* excludes us from the treatment that other members of the community of rational beings deserve and dictates the use of force, given that we are impervious to reason. The case of the Inquisition is particularly exemplary. The violence is that much more intense when it is not only physical. Beyond questioning the rationality of those who do not share their system of values, the absolutists, sheltered by the *objectivity* of their values to the point that all rational beings should assume them, exclude from the human community those who question these values.

In the end, to defend their values or their *form of life*, the relativist, as much as the absolutist, have recourse to the use of force when all of the arguments are exhausted. However, the radical difference lies in the fact that the absolutist feels *fully justified* to do so and that this violence is not their responsibility, as they limit themselves to being the docile instrument of the *Good* and of *Reason*.

If in relation to the question of ethics and moral values the opposition between relativism and absolutism is radical, it is no less intense as regards the question of truth.

The question of truth

Let us recall that the relativist does not say that "the truth does not exist", still less that "it is true that the truth does not exist", which would obviously be self-contradictory. They only say that the only thing which can be affirmed from the perspective of our way of thinking is that the truth "is", but that it is "conditioned"; that is, that it always depends on a certain merker or context.

No one, including the relativist, puts into question that, within a specific context, certain beliefs should be accepted as *true-in-that-context*. What the relativist rejects is that *the truth* constitutes a property which, for reasons of principle, transcends *any context*. This attitude represents a serious threat to two fundamental beliefs which the absolutists consider indispensable: the belief in the *universal* nature of truth and in its *objective* character.

Universalism affirms that true beliefs are so "at all times, in all contexts and for all human beings". The reference to *all times* means that nothing which occurs in the future can alter the truth of a proposition, if it is really *true*. The relativist sees no rational argument which can permit making wagers of this sort about the future and considers them the expression of a mere act of faith. As for the reference to *all contexts*, the relativist asks how anyone can come to know which contexts there are in *all* contexts. And as regards the reference to *all human beings*, the relativist is not only disposed to admit that *certain* truths hold effectively for all human beings, but sees in this fact a confirmation of their own point of view.

To the extent that all human beings share common characteristics—for example, of a biological type—it is not surprising then that certain truths hold for everyone. However, this precisely redounds to the idea that truth is relative to a determined marker which, in this case, are human characteristics. If these characteristics were different, there would continue to be valid truths for all human beings; but because the *context* would be different, these truths would be distinct from those currently held (to offer an example, it could be true that pure hydrochloric acid was good for our skin).

The second basic belief threatened by relativism is *objectivism*. That is, the belief that the truth is independent of the procedures which establish it or of any characteristic of who establishes it. According to *objectivism*, a belief is *true* if it transcends the particular point of view from which it was formulated, if it is abstracted from the marker within which it was produced, and if it is not affected by the location of who enunciated it. This signifies that it is true if it expresses, therefore, a point of view *from nowhere*, that is, a generic location without qualities. As the relativist cannot see how it is possible to accede to something in complete independence from how it is acceded to, neither can they see any meaning in *objectivism*, unless they accept the hypothesis that there exists a place that corresponds with the *point of view of God* and that we can put ourselves in this precise place.

The effort deployed by the absolutists to demonstrate the inanity of relativism does not limit itself to signaling its dangers for reason and putting into doubt its logical consistency. This effort also seeks to show the inconsistency of relativism in daily life, given that the relativist would be obliged to deny in practice what they proclaim in theory. In effect, however much the relativist attacks truth in theory, it is easy to verify that this contradicts what they do in practice. It is obvious that in their daily life, that the relativist has no remedy but to permanently invoke the criterion of truth, to employ profusely the *true/false* dichotomy and assume, firmly, the true character of a very ample ensemble of beliefs.

To be able to live, an individual has to believe in the existence of truth. Those human beings who would be incapable of distinguishing between true and false beliefs would extinguish themselves immediately, if they were abandoned to their own fate. This does not mean that human beings have no false beliefs, but it does imply that the majority of our beliefs must be true and that we have to discern them as such to be able to develop in the world. In other words, the use of the *true/false* dichotomy constitutes one of the conditions for the possibility of our experience and it forms an integral part of the conditions for the possibility of our very existence.

Whether we defend a relativist position or not, it is true that if we put our hand in the fire we burn ourselves, that certain plants are toxic and others comestible; it is true that the extermination camps existed, that 2+2=4, that gender, racial, class, etc. discrimination exist; it is true that we cannot do without the concept of the *truth*, and it is true that to deny the truth of all of this is properly untenable. There is therefore a contradiction between what the relativist affirms theoretically and what they do in practice.

A contradiction between theory and practice would in effect be produced if the relativist rejected the concept of truth on the level of theory, but they do not do so. Relativism does not intend to *abandon* the concept of truth, but only to give it a *new meaning*, distancing it from its absolutist conceptualisation and marking it pragmatically. What the relativist questions is not the pragmatic value of the belief in truth, but the philosophical presuppositions assumed by the absolutist in this belief.

The usefulness that the fact of believing in the truth represents is in no way put into doubt by the relativist. However, we cannot but remember that *usefulness as a value* presupposes nothing more than this, and that no *logical bridge* exists which allows us to move from *utility* to *truth*. That something is useful does not imply that it is true. Consequently, that we appeal in our daily life to an absolutist conception of truth tells us nothing about the true or false character of this conception.

For example, we all use the truth in the sense of *correspondence*, when we agree that "a statement about certain facts is true, if the facts are effectively as the statement says that they are". This way of using the truth is undoubtedly tremendously useful for our manner of relating to the world and, also, of dialoguing with others. Today, however, we all know that the correspondence notion of truth is logically and conceptually untenable, despite its doubtless utility.

When they play a game of chess, the relativist assumes an ensemble of rules: they assume, for example, that the proposition according to which the bishop can only move diagonally is true and that to accept it is part of the very possibility of playing chess. There is, however, no need to accept *anything further*, there is no need to accept that there is something like an *essence* of the game of chess or that there is something like a place where, independently of our decisions, the rules of chess are located.

The same occurs with the semantic rules of the absolutist type that govern the use of the true/false dichotomy. We have to assume these rules, to assure our existence; nevertheless, we do not have to commit ourselves to anything more than the unquestionable pragmatic value that the correct application of these rules has. Utility and truth are terms that refer to distinct conceptual fields; true and useful are predicates which do not function in the same semantic fields. The pragmatic value of truth only has value within the context of a specific *form of life* and for *the kind of being that we are*.

The relativist therefore defends a pragmatic conception of truth and recognises, furthermore, that in ordinary language the semantics of truth is of an absolutist kind, given that it fully assumes universalism and objectivism. Whether we wish it or not, absolutist type truth forms part of our use of the concept of truth in everyday life. This is comprehensible if we accept with Ludwig Wittgenstein that the grammar which governs any language must have a pragmatic value, that is, it must be such that it allows us to develop ourselves in the world. Language is in effect one of the principal tools elaborated by the human being to settle themself adequately within the surrounding world. But for this tool to have been effective, it had to connect to, join with, the characteristics of the world and, so to speak, these latter had to slowly inscribe themselves in our *grammar*. Accordingly, it is utility which presents the true/false distinction so that we could adapt to the world, the world as it would come to be reflected in our semantics of truth.

In the same way that our place in the world presupposes the existence of truth defined in absolute terms, the relation that we maintain with our fellows presents the same demands. However, this does not have to co-validate the absolutist conception of truth.

We cannot in effect *generate meaning*, if not within the setting of conventions and shared practices with our fellows, within a specific culture. Without this exchange and without this common background, communication would be totally impossible. In the same way that one cannot play chess without defining a certain number of rules valid for all players, neither can one communicate or exchange except in the context of a *game of rules* which constrains the acceptability of statements, thus impeding arbitrariness. The fact of admitting, as the relativist does, that these rules are purely conventional does not excuse us from following them if we intend to *play*, that is, in this case, to dialogue and to give meaning.

That the truth depends on our conventions does not mean that we can adopt this or that convention, according to our taste, because our practices and conventions are constrained by our characteristics, by our history and by the demands of life in common, especially those that concern communication. We are not authorised therefore to decide arbitrarily whatever we please to affirm as true. We cannot decide, for example, that a glass of sulfuric acid is good for our health, in the same way that we cannot decide that the extermination camps did not exist, because it was *so decided*. This would be to exclude oneself from any possibility of debate. If one intends to communicate with others, then arguments are necessary and the rules of argumentation have to be respected. To restore truth to our practices, to our conventions and to our characteristics does not mean to remit it to our free will. Relativism does not open the path to arbitrariness. Rather, it most certainly closes access to *arguments from authority* and demands that whatever is affirmed, including the existence of extermination camps, that it be argued for from within the framework of conventions made as explicit as possible. Just as considering truth in absolute terms was renounced, so it is necessary to define as precisely as possible the conditions in which this or that affirmation will be admitted as true, and this of course does not tolerate any exception.

In conclusion, relativism — which is only self-contradictory if it is evaluated according to the criteria *against which it constitutes itself*— does not end at any ethical precipice and does not lead to any political inhibition. On the contrary, it demands a commitment as combative as if it had opted for a specific normative position. In like manner, relativism does not disarm us before choices made and it does not render debate futile, but rather the opposite, given that it makes us responsible for our choices and forces us to defend them, arguing for them. In fact, it seems that ultimately all of the false complaints made against relativism cannot forgive what is most fundamental to it, namely, *a mortal blow dealt to the very principle of authority.* The existence of *Absolute Truths* and *Universal Values* bestows on whoever has them in their possession the right and, even, the moral obligation to vanquish whoever moves away from these truths and these values. In rising up against these absolutes, relativism finishes in a certain way the enterprise undertaken by the Enlightenment; and it is no longer just God, but its *doubles* as well, that see themselves expelled from human affairs.

Finally, I want to call attention to the fact, certainly clearly evident, that our relationship to the world is not exclusively, nor primarily, a relationship of knowledge, but that it is also a relationship of action, of encounters, of sensations, of experiences and sentiments. It is certain that

Plato contributed in an important way to privileging the *will to know* and to prioritising the *search for truth* above the remaining human practices. We however do not have to follow his footsteps. We can also question the privilege conceded to truth and prioritise an *ethics and an aesthetics of existence*, in the sense of constructing the possibility that all of us be able to create a beautiful life and one worthy of being lived.

It is obvious that for absolutism, *the Truth* offers no doubt. It is resplendent, brilliant, hard, unmistakable and overwhelming. Its edges appear clear, cutting, and they offer themselves to us in terms of *all or nothing*: *half-truths* were never *the Truth*. Truth is not negotiable, it holds for everyone and it holds for ever. Universal, atemporal, absolute, it is indisputable, it imposes itself. We can look away from it, refuse to recognise it, but the truth will continue to be the truth above our decisions. No posterior evidence can change it and, should it change the truth, it is because it was not really true, it only seemed to be. The truth is either absolute or it is not the truth, and when we find it and proclaim it, we are appropriating time and dominating the future; that is, denying it. The future can only show that a truth was not true, but if it is, nothing can go against it. The *will to Truth* is, directly, a *will to Power* that seeks, furthermore, to legislate for eternity. From this perspective, it constitutes a danger and a weakening of our freedom.

The truth is an epistemological question, the construction of the way of life that deserves to be lived is an ethical question. Between ethics and epistemology, the choice, as a significant part of anarchism seen with clarity, offers no doubts, because to decide *how we want to be* is considerably more important than asking ourselves: what can we know?

AFTERWORD

By editors Rob Ray and Scorsby

Anarchism is Movement is in many ways a drastically different book from our normal fare. As the oldest anarchist publishing house press in the English language, Freedom Press falls roundly into the category of "organised anarchism" that is so heavily critiqued throughout this work. Where Ibáñez rails against the "predominance of a cult of memory" strangling the joy of a living anarchism, we can only take a wry look at the latest catalogue, replete with its histories and republished classical theory. Our tradition was once described in 1897 as that of "fossilised old quill drivers"—we indeed have a long memory.

Our modern collective too, is by no means wedded to the sorts of theories over how and why movements grow, or our places within those movements, which Ibáñez describes and in some cases lauds in his consideration of where modern forms of anarchism are finding their stride. When he talks of the Occupy Movement and its successes in the context of "neoanarchism", many of our members and friends might raise a weary eyebrow, remembering ways in which the politics of St Pauls and Wall Street warped, withered and gathered a patina of intractable problems over their short lifetimes.

Some of this perspective is of course to do with how our environment moulds us. Organising a bookshop, or a small publishing house, running a building and trying to maintain a semblance of sustainable solidarity over years makes for grinding, often thankless work which encourages cynical practicality. Habits of structure can act to ground the lightning strike of spontaneous collective rebellion and in doing so, risk robbing such a moment of its vitality.

Some however is a vital aspect of the ecosystem of rebellion, helping ensure that when waves of activism recede we can raise them higher the next time. Those of us who run buildings are aware that one day soon they'll be needed again. Physical spaces beyond the reach of eviction notices are important bastions, and groups with long-running expertise can short-circuit painful relearnings of vital lessons. ACAB is not just a slogan, it is a structural critique that every new challenger to power must imbibe for their own safety. *The Tyranny of Structurelessness* isn't merely a well-turned line, it's the memory of a million hours lost on waffle and ego.

Arguments often break out within the movement over the importance of remembering our history compared to the need for engagement with the now, in all its messiness. In truth perhaps both the "organised" anarchists and Ibáñez's neoanarchists need each other, one wing offering support, stories of how the State's strategies of repression are constructed and a repository of tactical memory, the other offering opportunities to break from the inward turn, from ossified argumentation and disengaged paralysis.

The experience of Dave Douglass, a miner and flying picket in the strike of 1984 whose political journey led him to engage with almost every part of the left, from Stalinism to Posadism[45] to anarchism, may help to illustrate. In the first entry of his three-part autobiography, *Geordies — Wa Mental*, Dave describes growing up in a miners' world, a North Eastern union stronghold where the Communist Party was the starting point of any aspiring young red. The meaning of class solidarity was part of

---

45 A quite fantastic strain of 1960s Trotskyism in which impending nuclear doom was considered a great revolutionary opportunity and UFOs the potential advance guard of a communist space empire that should be encouraged to intervene for the sake of humanity's glorious socialist future.

his upbringing. But it was when he and his mates ran into the peace movement's beatnik generation — the Committee of 100, Aldermaston, CND and the rise of the hippies — that revolution became *fun*:

> "The world changed from the black and white, or grey, of the Young Communist League's brand of Marxism to a spinning top of whirling technicolour … This fusion of the Bigg Market ILPers, the beats, the hip freaks, the pacifists and the anarchists carried a sacred glow of mystery and, with me basking in that glow, it was the day the circus hit town."

Variations of Douglass's story can be found ten thousand times over in the tales of those who have committed to the ideals of anarchism. From new age travelers to rave culture and climate carnivals, the possibilities of a space to explore freedom, build radical new communities, learn about yourself and others — and have a good time — have nurtured blooms of libertarian radicalism in multiple generations.

It should be possible to marry the joy of rebellion with the needs and long term goals of organised class struggle. To encourage a situation such as that of 1984, where striking miners were laughing along with *Class War*'s bloodthirsty insurrectionary hyperbole in between mass meetings of the pickets.

Anarchism is Movement nods at such sentiments while containing occasional either-ors which are perhaps overstated, and the demarcation of anarchist "types" is prominent among them. Within our own little collective are punkish squatters, leaners towards insurrectionism, stolid syndicalists and autonomists, younger and less so. Our reasons for membership in this oldest of organisations are manifold, our friendships and connections wide. We can characterise with broad sweeps the tendencies within anarchism, at the rhetorical grappling between dour workerists, flighty opportunists, conflictual romantics — but it is equally important to remember that below the relative calm of categorisation there is ever a teeming mass of collaboration and (self) contradiction.

This is of course a natural problem when taking such an overview and snapshot of any movement, and shouldn't take away from the impact of this work. Ibáñez is a hugely creative thinker and the thrust of his argument is well worth engaging with. In defining himself as being at war with "the guardians of the temple" he argues strongly for a more positive attitude towards what he views as the revitalisation of a living and evolving anarchist praxis where people are, in liberatory spirit, chewing away at the pillars of social oppression whenever space can be found.

Ibáñez's ultimate argument, that anarchists must reconcile to the realities of the present rather than hold to utopian dreams of a future imagined by the minds of a century prior, paradoxically mirrors some of the views espoused by those he criticises.

One of the most famous images of the syndicalist IWW union features a man in overalls pointing at a factory shouting "Organise!" while anarchists, socialists and Marxists gaze to the heavens in front of him. It is as neat a summary of the syndicalist (and anarcho-syndicalist) view of the time as you could wish for. The aim was to challenge capitalism at the point where it was weakest, where the worker had direct power to cross their arms and cease co-operating with their masters.

Today however such aims have run up against a high wall. With industry outsourced or virtualised worldwide—and sometimes entirely automated—power at the point of production requires a level of class co-operation across borders and physical boundaries that has proven slippery at best and as a result, even base trade unionism can struggle to cope outside a few skilled, unmovable industries (transport, public service etc). The idea of us all folding our arms and making the factories stop seems remote, and while production remains the ultimate cornerstone which must be wrested from under capitalism to make it fall, that breeds an obsession over exactly how the defences can be breached.

Ibáñez, a man who himself looked at one stage to the post-Franco Spanish CNT as a great hope for revolution's rebirth, thus looks to find the weak points that can be reached now, amid the doldrums of a workers' movement that can sometimes seem smothered by its own fading banners. And in espousing anarchism as a living tendency with a fluidity of tactics, alongside a tacit acknowledgement that the working class fights not just for bread but roses too, he asks questions of our times that stand consideration.

~ **Rob Ray**

***

While editing *Anarchism is Movement* I shifted between nodding my head vigorously and pausing, disconcerted, over his ideas so frequently I almost got whiplash. As an insurrectionary anarchist turned organised anarchist (through my work with Freedom) I have often pondered whether this shift does indeed constitute a "turn" theoretically, or in fact is just the application of a consistent ideology onto changing circumstances. *Anarchism is Movement* does much to legitimise such a belief.

The strength of his text is its willingness to attempt to constitute and conceptualise a way in which different anarchistic tendencies are not in fact in opposition to each other nor fighting for primacy but that embraces the diversity of the modern anarchistic moment. His optimism is sometimes overegged but, in the face of the often wearying cynicism and tendency towards defeatism on the anarchist left, deeply refreshing.

By framing the new activisms of the last decade as inclusive of anarchist practices and ideologies without framing themselves so, he creates a space for a broader interpretation of anarchism, focusing on practices as much as theories. While this sometimes appears contradictory, such as in his determination that anarchism began only at the point in which it was conceived as such, it also allows us to see the "resurgence and renewal" of anarchism as he refers to the new anarchist "wave", in multiple instances and moments of rebellion, whether or not they are wholesale described or identified as such.

This is also observed in his approach towards internet-age activism, which he sees as having great potential for inspiring and communicating alternative radical politics, as well as part of a broader epoch shift in understandings and practices of anarchism, following on from 1968. By highlighting and celebrating what he sees as anarchistic tendencies or action occurring in a multitude of events and moments of coming together he avoids the rigid demarcation of this or that moment being deemed anarchist or not.

This optimism may be read by some as unfounded or naïve, but by centering the importance of the constitution of the political subject and the effect generated by engagement in radical struggle he helps us to remember why and how we all came to be anarchists. Not through theories and heavy texts (though they help) but more often through engagements in struggle, which offered an idea of what an alternative way of living, of being, could be like, and allowed us to hope and to act in order to bring it about both in the future and in the here and now.

While at times he flirts with a definitional rigidity that verges on ranking different anarchist tendencies against each other, he always comes back to the eponymous point: anarchism is movement. It is flexible, changeable, adaptable, and while you may ascribe yourself to one tendency or another, this does not alter that fact that the overall potential of anarchism is larger, greater, and more malleable than that—and this is, fundamentally, its strength.

~ **Scorsby**

ACKNOWLEDGEMENTS
(FROM THE SPANISH EDITION)

If it were not for the friendship and wisdom of Félix Vázquez, my Gallicisms and other grammatical and stylistic incongruities would have turned this book into a cruel linguistic affront. Many thanks, Félix, for the rigorous revision and the sensible suggestions. Were it not for the hope and the commitment of so many anarchists who gave their lives for this idea and the continuous, enthusiastic passion of those who continue to animate it, it is obvious that this book could simply not have been, and therefore my thanks also go to the broad libertarian horizon that has made it possible, and within it, I can't fail to mention the collective that has continued to maintain, with its dedication and efforts, the Virus publisher.

BIBLIOGRAPHY

ADAMS, Jason (2003): "Postanarchism in a Nutshell". Published also with the title: Postanarchism in a Bombshell. *Aporia Journal*, 2.

BEY, Hakim (1987): "Post-Anarchism Anarchy". In Rousselle, Duane and Evren, Süreyya (Eds): *Post-Anarchism: A Reader*. London: Pluto Press, 2011.

– (1987): "Ontological Anarchy in a Nutshell". In Bey, Hakim. *Immediatism. Essays by Hakim Bey*. Edinburgh: AK Press, 1994.

– (1990): *TAZ: The Temporary Autonomous Zone, Ontological Anarchy, Poetic Terrorism*. New York: Autonomedia, 2003.

BERTI, Giampietro (2012): *Libertà senza rivoluzione. L'anarchismo fra la sconfitta del comunismo e la vittoria del capitalismo*. Roma: Piero Lacaita Editore.

BLACK, Bob (1997): *Anarchy After Leftism. The Anarchist Library*. Available at: https://theanarchistlibrary.org/library/bob-black-anarchy-after-leftism.

BOOKCHIN, Murray (1995): *Social Anarchism or Lifestyle Anarchism: An Unbridgeable Chiasm*. Edinburgh: AK Press.

CALL, Lewis (2002): *Postmodern Anarchism*. Lanham: Lexington Books.

COHN, Jesse and WILBUR, Shawn (2003): "What's Wrong with Postanarchism?". *The Anarchist Library*. Available at: https://theanarchistlibrary.org/library/jesse-cohn-and-shawn-wilbur-what-s-wrong-with-postanarchism.

DAY, Richard (2005): *Gramsci is Dead. Anarchist Currents in the Newest Social Movements*. London: Pluto Press.

FERRER, Christian (Comp.) (1990): *El lenguaje libertario*. Montevideo: Nordan-Comunidad.

– (2004): *Cabezas de tormenta. Ensayos sobre lo ingobernable*. Logroño: Pepitas de calabaza.

FRANKS, Benjamin (2007): "Postanarchism: a critical assessment". *Journal of Political Ideologies*, 12(2), 127-145.

GARCIA, Vivien (2007): *L'anarchism aujourd'hui*. Paris: L'Harmattan.

GEE, Teoman (2003): *New anarchism: some thoughts*. Alpine Anarchist Productions.

GLAVIN, Michael (2004): Power, Subjectivity, Resistance: Three Works on Postmodern Anarchism". *New Formulation*, 2(2). Available at: http://www.cwmorse.org/archives/New-Formulation-2-2.pdf.

GORDON, Uri (2005): *Anarchism and Political Theory: Contemporary problems*. Oxford: University of Oxford. Available at *The Anarchist Library*: https://theanarchistlibrary.org/ library/uri-gordon-anarchism-and-political-theory-contemporary-problems.

– (2008): *Anarchy Alive! Anti-Authoritarian Politics from Practice to Theory*. London: Pluto Press.

GRAEBER; David (2002): "The New Anarchists". *New Left Review*, 13, 61-73. Available at: https://newleftreview.org/issues/II13/articles/david-graeber-the-new-anarchists.

– (2013): *Oltre il potere e la burocrazia, l'immaginazione contro la violenza, l'ignoranza e la stupidità*. Milán: Elèuthera.

JUN, Nathan J. (2012): *Anarchism and Political Modernity*. New York: Continuum.

KOCH, Andrew M. (1993): "Poststructuralism and the Epistemological Basis of Anarchism". *Philosophy of the Social Sciences*. 23(3), 327-351. In Rousselle, Duane and Evren, Süreyya (Eds): *Post-Anarchism: A Reader*. London: Pluto Press, 2011. Available at: https://theanarchistlibrary.org/library/ andrew-m-koch-poststructuralism-and-the-epistemological-basis-of-anarchism.

KUHN, Gabriel (2009): "Anarchism, Postmodernity and Poststructuralism". In Amster, Randall; DeLeon, Abraham; Fernandez, Luis; Nocella, II, Anthony J. and Shannon, Deric (Eds.): *Contemporary Anarchist Studies: An Introductory Anthology of Anarchism in the Academy*. Abingdon: Routledge.

MOORE, John (1997): "Anarchism and Poststructuralism". *Anarchist Studies*. 5(2), 157-161.

MORLAND, David (2004): "Anti-capitalism and Poststructuralist Anarchism". In Purkis, Jonathan and Bowen, James (Eds.): *Changing Anarchism: Anarchist Theory and Practice in a Global Age*. Manchester: Manchester University Press.

NEWMAN, Saul (2001): *From Bakunin to Lacan: Anti-Authoritarianism and the Dislocation of Power*. Lanham: Lexington Books.

– (2010): *The Politics of Postanarchism*. Edinburgh: Edinburgh University Press.

– (2013): *Fantasie rivoluzionarie e zone autonome, post-anarchismo e spazio*. Milán: Elèuthera.

ONFRAY, Michel (2013): *Il post-anarchismo spiegato e mia nonna*. Milàn: Elèuthera.

PURKIS, Jonathan and BOWEN, James (Eds.) (1997): Twenty-First Century Anarchism: Unorthodox Ideas for a New Millennium. London: Cassell.

– (Eds.) (2004) *Changing Anarchism: Anarchist Theory and Practice in a Global Age*. Manchester: Manchester University Press.

ROUSSELLE, Duane and EVREN, Süreyya (Eds) (2011): *Post-Anarchism: A Reader*. London: Pluto Press.

SCHMIDT, Michael and VAN DER WALT, Lucien (2009): *Black Flame. The Revolutionary Class Politics of Anarchism and Syndicalism*. Oakland: AK Press.

TODD, May (1989): "Is Post-Structuralist Political Theory Anarchist?". *Philosophy and Social Criticism*, 15(2), 167-182.

BIBLIOGRAPHY135
BIBLIOGRAPHY

- (1994): *The Political Philosophy of Poststructuralist Anarchism*. University Park: Pennsylvania State University Press.

TURKELI, Süreyya (2012): *What is Anarchism? A Reflection on the Canon and The Constructive Potential of Its Destruction*. Doctoral Thesis. Loughborough University.

VACCARO, Salvo (coord.) (2011): *Pensare altrimenti, anarchismo e filosofia radicale del novecento*. Milán, Eléuthera.

WARD, Colin (1973): *Anarchy in Action*. London: Allen and Unwin.

ZERZAN, John (1991): "The Catastrophe of Postmodernism". *Anarchy: A Journal of Desire Armed*, 30, 16-25.

I also want to mention in this bibliography the following excellent journals:

A contretemps: http://acontretemps.org/

Anarchist Developments in Cultural Studies: https://journals.uvic.ca/index.php/adcs/index

Anarchist Studies: https://www.lwbooks.co.uk/anarchist-studies

Réfractions: http://refractions.plusloin.org/

Publications by the author used in or related to the text

a. Books

1982. *Poder y Libertad*. Barcelona: Hora.

2001. *Municiones para disidentes*. Barcelona: Gedisa.

2005. *Contra la dominación*: Gedisa. Italian edition: *Il libero pensiero. Elogio del relativismo*. Milán: Eleuthera, 2007.

2006. *¿Por qué A?: fragmentos dispersos para un anarquismo sin dogmas*. Barcelona: Anthropos. Revised new edition (2007): *Actualidade del anarquismo*. Buenos Aires: Terramar Ediciones e Libros de Anarres (Ciolección Utopía Libertaria). Revised French edition (2010): *Fragments épars pour un anarchisme sans dogmes*. Paris: Rue des Cascades.

b. Selected articles

1981. "La inevitabilidad del poder político y la resistible ascención del poder coercitivo", *El Viejo Topo*, 60, 28-33. Republished in (2006): *¿Por qué A?: fragmentos dispersos para un anarquismo sin dogmas*. French edition (2010): *Fragments épars pour un anarchisme sans dogmes*.

1983. "Per un potere politico libertario", *Voluntà*, 3. Republished under the title: "Pour un pouvoir politique libertaire", en *Considérations épistémologiques et stratégiques autour d'un concept*. In Bertolo, Amedeo; Di Leo, Roosella; Colombo, Eduardo; Ibáñez, Tomás and Lourau, René (1984): *Le Pouvoir et sa négation*. Lyon: Atelier de Création Libertaire. Spanish edition (2006): *¿Por qué A?: fragmentos dispersos para un anarquismo sin dogmas*. French edition (2010): *Fragments épars pour un anarchisme sans dogmes*. There is also a Greek version published in 1992.

1985. "Addio à la rivoluzione", *Voluntà*, 1. French edition: AA.VV (1986): *La Révolution. Un anarchisme contemporain—Venise 84. Vol. IV.* Lyon: Atelier de Création Libertaire. Spanish edition (1986): *Utopía*, 6 (Buenos Aires); in Ferrer, Christian (Comp.) (1990): *El lenguaje libertario*, Vol. I. Montevideo: Nordan-Comunidad, and in (1999): *El lenguaje libertario. Antología*, Buenos Aires: Altamira. English version (1989): *Autonomy*, 1. Available at: http://autonomies.org/2010/04/farewell-to-the-revolution/.

1990. "Adiós a la revolución ... y ¡viva la gran desbarajuste!". Archipiélago, 4. Republished in (2006): *¿Por qué A?: fragmentos dispersos para un anarquismo sin dogmas*. French edition (2010): *Fragments épars pour un anarchisme sans dogmes*.

1993. "Sísifo y el centro, o la constante creación del orden y del poder por parte de quienes lo cuestionamos", *Archipiélago*, 13. Italian version (1992): *Voluntà*, 1. Republished in (2006): *¿Por qué A?: fragmentos dispersos para un anarquismo sin dogmas* and in (2007) *Actualidad del anarquismo*. French edition (2010): *Fragments épars pour un anarchisme sans dogmes*. There is also a Greek version.

1994. "Tutta la verità sul relativismo autentico", Voluntà, 2-3. French version: AA.VV (1997): *Tout est relatif. Peut être.* Lyon: Atelier de Création Libertaire. Spanish version (2006): *¿Por qué A?: fragmentos dispersos para un anarquismo sin dogmas* and in (2007) *Actualidad del anarquismo*. French edition (2010): *Fragments épars pour un anarchisme sans dogmes*.

1996. "Questa idea si conjuga all'imperfetto", *Voluntà*, 3-4. Spanish version (2006): *¿Por qué A?: fragmentos dispersos para un anarquismo sin dogmas* and in (2007) *Actualidad del anarquismo*. French edition (2010): *Fragments épars pour un anarchisme sans dogmes*.

2001. "Instalados en la provisionalidad y en el cambio ... (¡Como la vida misma!)", *Libre Pensamiento*, 37-38. French version (2002): "Installé entre le provisoire et le changement, comme la vie elle-même". *IRL—Informations Rassemblées à Lyon*, 90. Republished in (2006): *¿Por qué A?: fragmentos dispersos para un anarquismo sin dogmas* and in (2007) *Actualidad del anarquismo*.

2002. "¿Es actual el anarquiso?", *Página Abierta*, 123. Republished in (2003): *La lletra A*, 61. Portuguese version (2004): *Utopia*, 18. French version (2006): *A Contretemps*, 24 and in (2010): *Fragments épars pour un anarchisme sans dogmes*. Republished in (2006): *¿Por qué A?: fragmentos dispersos para un anarquismo sin dogmas* and in (2007) *Actualidad del anarquismo*.

2006. "A Contratiempo", *Libre Pensamiento*, 51. Republished in (2006): *¿Por qué A?: fragmentos dispersos para un anarquismo sin dogmas* and in (2007) *Actualidad del anarquismo*. French edition (2010): *Fragments épars pour un anarchisme sans dogmes*.

2006. "A l'aube du XXI siècle: les clairs-obscures de la nouvelle donne", Réfraction, 17. Spanish version (2007): Libre Pensamiento, 55, and in (2007) *Actualidad del anarquismo*. Also in (2010): *Fragments épars pour un anarchisme sans dogmes*.

2007. "Neoanarquismo e società contemporanea. Diálogo com Manuel Castells", *Libertaria*, 1-2. Original version in Castilian (2008): "El neoanarquismo, la libertad y la sociedad contemporánea. Diálogo con Manuel Castells", *Archipiélago*, 83-84. There also exists a version published in Greece.

2008. "Points de vue sur l'anarchisme (et aperçus sur le néo-anarchisme et le post-anarchisme)", *Réfractions*, 20. Italian version (2008): *Libertaria*, 3-4. There is also a version published in Greece. French version (2010): *Fragments épars pour un anarchisme sans dogmes*.

2009. "Los nuevos códigos de la dominación y de las luchas", *Libre Pensamiento*, 62. Italian version (2009): "Le nuove forme del dominio e delle lotte", *Libertaria*, 4. French version (2010): *Fragments épars pour un anarchisme sans dogmes*.

2009. "Il post-anarchismo e il neo-anarchismo" (text for the Colloquium of Marghera) and "Apuntes sobre neoanarquismo" (text for the Colloquium of Pisa), *Bollettino Archivio G. Pinelli*, 34. There is also a Greek version (2010): *Eutopía*, 18, 2011, and in French: "Conversations avec Tomás Ibáñez", *A Contretemps*, 39.

2011. "Pouvoir et liberté: une tension inhérente au champ politique", *Réfractions*, 27.

2011. "La Rivoluzione". In AA.VV: *Rivoluzione?* Milán: Asperimenti. Spanish version (2012): "La revolución", *Libre Pensamiento*, 70. There is also a version published in Greece.

2011. "El 15M y la tradición libertaria", *Polémica*, 100.

2012. "Le temps saccadé des révoltes", *Réfractions*, 28. Spanish version (2012): El sorprendente ritmo de las revueltas", *Libre Pensamiento*, 71.

2012. "L'anarchisme est un type d'être constitutivement changeant. Arguments pour un neo-anarchisme". In Angaut, Jean-Christophe; Colson, Daniel and Pucciarelli, Mimmo (Eds.): *Philosophie de l'anarchie. Théories libertaires, practiques quotidiennes et ontologie*. Lyon: Atelier de Création Libertaire.

2013. "La raison governementale at les métamorphoses de l'État", *Réfractions*, 3.

ALSO FROM FREEDOM...

Anarchism without
the syndicalism

£5

Anarchism in the
everyday

£7.50

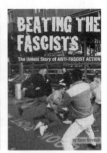

Red Action on the
1980s street war

£15

Loveable cartoon and
class struggle

£8

George Barrett's
intro to anarchism

£7.50

Radical memoir by
Albert Meltzer

£7

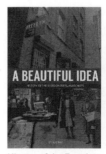

History of the Freedom
Press Anarchists

£9.50

A year of rough sleeping
in stories and essays

£10

Mental health guide
for activists

£4